THE GIFTS OF CAREGIVING

Stories of Hardship, Hope, and Healing

CONNIE GOLDMAN

Fairview Press
in cooperation with the
Center for Spirituality and Healing,
University of Minnesota, Minneapolis

Published by Fairview Press, 2450 Riverside Avenue, Minneapolis, Minnesota 55454, in cooperation with the Center for Spirituality and Healing, University of Minnesota. Fairview Press is a division of Fairview Health Services, a community-focused health system, affiliated with the University of Minnesota, providing a complete range of services, from the prevention of illness and injury to care for the most complex medical conditions.

The Center for Spirituality and Healing

Established in 1995 at the University of Minnesota, the Center for Spirituality and Healing is a nationally recognized leader in mind-body medicine and brings together bio-medical, complementary, cross-cultural, and spiritual aspects of patient care. For more information, go to www.csh.umn.edu.

Library of Congress Cataloging-in-Publication Data
The gifts of caregiving : stories of hardship, hope, and healing / [compiled by] Connie Goldman.
         p. cm.
ISBN 1-57749-117-3 (trade paperback : alk. paper)
1. Caregivers—Biography. 2. Handicapped—Home care—Case studies. 3. Aged—Home care—Case studies. 4. Terminally ill—Home care—Case studies. I. Goldman, Connie.
HV1552.3.G54 2002
649.8'092'2—dc21   2002007089

First Printing: September 2002

Printed in Canada
05 04 03 02   5 4 3 2 1

Cover: *Laurie Ingram Design*

For a free current catalog of Fairview Press titles, please call toll-free 1-800-544-8207. Or visit our Web site at www.fairviewpress.org.

CONTENTS

Isak Dinesen once said that all the sorrows of life are bearable if only we can convert them into stories. This book is a collection of stories about caregivers, and the collection helps us to see how hardship can be converted into hope. But the magical power of this conversion remains hidden from us, a mystery we have not yet begun to unravel.

Paradoxically, this magic is hidden in plain sight because the stories themselves are so clear and powerful that they speak immediately to the heart. We read the stories and are moved to tears. We recognize simple goodness, we are inspired by acts of kindness, and we come away even envying the storytellers, these remarkable people who cope with adversity in ways that leave us wondering: "Could I measure up to this challenge?"

What is hidden from us—the conversion of hardship into hope—is a mysterious element in the hearts of caregivers, an element that permits one person's caregiving to be a kind of alchemy, transforming a base metal into gold, while another, faced with a similar challenge, comes away embittered and exhausted. What accounts for this difference? What power in our own hearts could permit us to respond in such different ways to the imperative duties and impossible demands of caregiving?

The inspirational stories you will read in this book are other people's stories, and each one is unique. They cover a territory as wide as caregiving itself: from birth defects to Alzheimer's disease, from spousal obligation to volunteer caregiving, from anguish to triumph.

The word "inspirational" may conjure up images of romantic glory—of someone like Mother Theresa rising from the slums of Calcutta to receive the Nobel Peace Prize—when we know too well that much of what is called caregiving is drudgery, loneliness, and boredom. Above all, it is largely invisible. Caregivers are seldom celebrated in the public arena. How do we cope with this invisibility? We don't need to become world-renowned heroes, but each of us must find our own path, our own magical element, the alchemy that helps us escape resentment and frustration and find the gold in our own heart.

Each of us, if we live long enough, can reasonably expect to encounter a caregiving challenge. Caregiving is our universal destiny. There are very few people who will reach advanced old age without being afflicted by chronic illness. All of us, as family or friends, will be touched by at least one person whose affliction falls into the category of hardship. We don't like to think about this fact, and so our current cultural infatuation with "Successful Aging" and "Vital Aging" insists that we keep these demons at bay.

Perhaps our cultural messages are wrong. Perhaps there are important lessons to be learned from caregiving, lessons about vulnerability, about our shared dependence on "the kindness of strangers," about giving up illusions of control and autonomy. Both the one who is cared for and the one who gives the care face a challenge. Will we measure up? When our time comes, how will we respond to the challenge at hand?

If we think of life as a journey, then the condition of dependency can at any time interrupt our forward movement on this journey. A sudden stroke or a car crash, and life changes in an instant. We can't help but think: "It could have been me." Instead of a far-off destination, the journey suddenly becomes right here, in this bed, in this room, at this time. The journey of life, the forward movement, was perhaps always an illusion. When illusions fall away, we look for a new kind of hope. And the storytellers can provide us with that hope.

Journalists, like Connie Goldman, are constantly reminded to "get the story straight." In turn, they remind us to get our stories straight: not to lie, not to deceive ourselves. The old-fashioned virtue of truth-telling is the highest calling of the journalist, who is first and last a storyteller. What this collection of stories helps us to do is get straight about the story of our own lives by reading the inspiring stories of those who have gone before us on the journey. For the transforming power of these stories we can only be grateful.

Harry R. Moody, Ph.D.
Senior Associate, International Longevity Center-USA

This book began as a radio program. In early 1999, I produced a one-hour special for public radio called "Hardship into Hope: The Rewards of Caregiving." The program consisted of a series of interviews with family caregivers—some well known and some not so well known, but all with inspiring stories to share. A copy of this program, recorded on a CD, has been attached to the inside back cover of this book.

After "Hardship into Hope" aired, I was overwhelmed with letters, e-mails, and phone calls from people across the nation, requesting printed transcripts and audiocassette recordings of the program. Listeners were inspired by the thoughtful words of Dana Reeve, wife and caregiver to actor Christopher Reeve, who suffered paralyzing spinal injuries in 1995. And by the insights of Ram Dass, the well-known spiritual leader whose stroke reversed his role of caregiver to care recipient. They resonated with former First Lady Rosalynn Carter's observation that nearly all of us will need a caregiver, or need to become a caregiver, sometime in our life. And they were grateful to hear positive stories of caregiving—stories of family intimacy, personal fulfillment, and spiritual growth.

Many of the listeners urged me to write a book based on the radio program. With their encouragement, I began to conduct additional interviews that put into words the special gifts of caregiving. The result is the book you hold in your hands: *The Gifts of Caregiving: Stories of Hardship, Hope, and Healing.*

When we read a book, we "hear" the words in our own voice, in our own head. But to be exposed to the actual voices of those telling their own stories, to actually hear people describing their experiences and feelings in their own words, offers a very different experience. Lane Stiles—my editor at Fairview Press—and I decided to provide you with both the printed and spoken word. The CD is not the book recorded. The book is not the radio program transcribed. Each is a separate experience. It makes no difference whether you read the book first and then listen to the CD, or listen first and then read. Our wish for you is that each will bring you information and inspiration—that you or someone you know will be supported in transforming the hardship of caregiving into hope and healing.

Connie Goldman
September 2002

INTRODUCTION

Many years ago I read ten words that shaped the direction of my career as a public radio producer, writer, and speaker. The poet Muriel Rukeyser wrote, "The world isn't made of atoms, it's made of stories." I had always been enchanted and entertained by a story. Thinking about the stories I had heard in my childhood and young adult years, I realized that in listening to these tales I had discovered things about myself, my feelings, and my values. We learn about ourselves from hearing the stories of others. Listening to other people tell their stories, we laugh, we cry, we empathize. A story in a magazine or a newspaper deeply touches us. In sharing a personal and poignant tale, someone totally unrelated to our own situation may offer us an unexpected source of comfort and inspiration. We can gain insight and wisdom from someone we don't know and may never meet. Such is the power of a story, and that is why I'm sharing caregivers' stories with you in this book.

The personal narratives you'll read came from my meetings with a variety of family caregivers in various parts of the country. I talked with many middle-aged children dealing with aging, often critically ill parents. Some of my conversations were with spouses or companions whose mates were deteriorating physically and mentally. I collected stories that parents told about one or more of their children who required special care, and in some cases would continue to require over their entire lifetime. I tape-recorded the experiences of people who had been caregivers for partners with AIDS; talked with family members who took care of cousins, aunts, or uncles; met with those who had assumed responsibility for the care of a friend; and spoke with several people who had taken over the care of a family member who lived a great distance away.

We learn about ourselves from hearing the stories of others.

I traveled to New Jersey to hear the story of a woman who gave up her business and home and moved across the country to care for her frail and ailing mother. I went to upstate New York to talk with a couple caring for two daughters who have been blind and physically limited since birth. And I met with a man in Maryland who lovingly cared for his wife as cancer drained her vitality. In Minneapolis I spoke with a woman who willingly assumed the role of family caregiver, first to care for her mother, then both her aunt and uncle. Why? The answer for her was simple: "I knew that if my mother were still alive she'd be doing this for others in the family. I felt it was my responsibility to take over." A friend of mine in Maryland described in some detail what she labeled "a miracle of healing" between herself and her dying mother. A lifetime of abrasive and argumentative contact had evolved into unselfish caring, mutual respect, and deep love. I don't underestimate the healing power of such stories.

Twenty-five years ago, when my mother became ill and partially dependent, the word *caregiver* didn't exist. As nearly as I can determine, it wasn't in the dictionary until 1997. I didn't think of myself as a caregiver, but simply as a daughter who, when her mother required help, would figure out how to provide the care that was needed. In my particular situation, my daughter and I became a caregiving team. She lived a short distance from her grandmother, while I lived and worked almost two thousand miles away. I made the major decisions, provided suggestions from a distance, and flew back to my hometown nearly every Friday to relieve my daughter until I had to leave on Monday.

I remember wishing I knew someone else who was a caregiver so I could talk about it with them. In my circle of friends, I was the first middle-aged daughter to take care of an aging parent. My friends wanted to help, but my particular situation was out of the realm of their experience. I constantly juggled fear, frustration, irritation, indecision, and guilt that I wasn't doing enough for my mother and that I shouldn't be living on the other side of the country during her time of need. At the end of her life, the most difficult thing for me was the sadness I felt, not only because of the loss, but because some of the misunderstandings and unresolved issues between my mother and myself were never openly discussed or repaired. Perhaps if I had heard stories of mother-daughter reconciliations, I could have put some of my anxieties to rest long ago.

I didn't think of myself as a caregiver, but simply as a daughter who, when her mother required help, would figure out how to provide the care that was needed.

During the years that followed the death of my mother, I talked with friends and family members about my pain and sadness over the fact that there had been no healing of our relationship. Our life together included lies, anger, hurt, and disappointment. Over the years, neither of us found a way to face these things, let them go, or reach out to each other with love. In the two decades since her death, people have told me many stories of difficult mother-daughter relationships that healed through caregiving. I've read several, collected some for my radio programs and books, and talked with people who have their own caregiver stories to tell. Their stories have given me the gift of healing. Forgiveness, compassion, acceptance, and love grow through empathy for and understanding of the experiences of others.

Family caregivers often feel burdened, overwhelmed, and stressed. There's a good chance that a person who has taken on the responsibility of caring for another will experience feelings of depression, helplessness, and isolation. Yet, we are far from alone. Dana Reeve, wife of actor Christopher Reeve who suffered paralyzing spinal cord injuries, told me: "One of the things that I've realized is that I'm part of a group called 'caregivers,' and there are millions of us. It's often something that we take on willingly because we love the person and because we feel it's our duty, and yet we don't see it as a job, necessarily, and it really is. Not that we wouldn't do it anyway."

Forgiveness, compassion, acceptance, and love grow through empathy for and understanding of the experiences of others.

Millions of us are currently providing care and assistance to someone who is ill, frail, or disabled, or we have done so in the past. This book is about these caregivers—wives, husbands, life partners, mothers, fathers, daughters, sons, sisters, brothers, cousins, friends, neighbors—anyone who takes on the responsibility of providing care and comfort for another's needs. Many times I've heard the figure quoted that only 5 percent of those requiring care are living in facilities that provide professional services. The other 95 percent live in their home or in the home of a relative. Their care has been taken on by family members or friends for whom caregiving isn't a paying job or a chosen career. An estimated twenty-five million adults have added a volunteer caregiving commitment to an already full life.

We most often become caregivers through unforeseen and unplanned-for circumstances. A father falls suddenly ill, a mother becomes increasingly forgetful, a spouse is diagnosed with a terminal illness, a grandmother is too frail to care for herself, an elderly friend is without family or resources, a child is born with severe physical or mental limitations. With little or no warning, we become caregivers.

We take on the role of caregiver because the alternatives aren't acceptable to our families or ourselves. Often we don't know what we're getting into, but we make the leap anyway, take on the responsibility, and hope for the best. Our day

We most often become caregivers through unforeseen and unplanned-for circumstances.

often includes dealing with frustration, stress, irritation, exhaustion, confusion, and guilt. Yet, sadness and uncertainty are only part of the experience. Caregiving is also about knowing we've done our best and served someone we love.

Along with an awareness that a cure might not be possible and an acceptance of what can't be controlled or changed, many of us learn something deeply meaningful and profoundly spiritual about ourselves. Through the caregiving experience we can expand our vision, touch new depths of compassion and gratitude, and reassess our priorities. A daughter, herself in her sixties, shared with me some thoughts as she reflected back on the time when she sat with her dying, semiconscious mother. "Hard as it all had been taking charge of her personal care, seeing my own living patterns changed in almost every conceivable way, struggling with the guilt of never doing enough, still in some way I can't really explain there's been some immeasurable value for me in just being there for her. Through this experience of caregiving, I think I've really grown and learned a lot about myself."

Many people I spoke with shared similar thoughts about a deepening personal awareness and growing sensitivity. Beth Witrogen McLeod, sitting in her sunny living room in Northern California, told me: "I think the ultimate learning in the giving of ourselves is that we find out who we are at heart. To give beyond any conceivable level than we ever thought we were capable of, or wanted to be capable of, or were willing to be capable of, is such a stretch of the heart. Still, the opportunity to give to someone—that is the most healing, the most glorious connection that we can have as a human. You can't help but see the world differently. It changes you profoundly and permanently. It's a constant lesson to find out who we truly are." Beth wrote about her caregiving experience with her parents in her book, *Caregiving as a Spiritual Journey.*

Along with an awareness that a cure might not be possible and an acceptance of what can't be controlled or changed, many of us learn something deeply meaningful and profoundly spiritual about ourselves.

In our conversations, the caregivers often told me how their priorities had changed—how they had gained new perspectives of what was meaningful in their lives and learned to slow down the pace of their days. Many spoke with a newfound sense of peace. I recall visiting with Gordon Dickman in Seattle. I was working on a totally different project at the time, and our appointment had nothing to do with caregiving. Yet, halfway through our conversation, Gordon shared an anecdote about his father's death. "This is a story about holding an angel that I didn't know was an angel," he began.

"My father wasn't a man of words. He never said, 'I love you,' or 'Son, you did a good job,' or sat down and shared heart-to-heart talks with me. So when he was in the last days of his life and comatose, and I was lying in bed with him holding him in my arms, I thought, 'Why am I holding you in my arms like this? Why am I doing things for you that you never did for me?' And I began to reflect, during that long day until he died, on all the things he had done for me.

"He'd driven miles when I was a child to take me to movies that I wanted to see. When I first started dating and couldn't drive a car, he'd driven into town, picked up the girl, taken us to the movies, gone somewhere and waited, come back and picked us up, and taken her home. And he never complained, never said no.

"He's the one who drove me to college, set my trunk out at the corner, and drove off and waited at the end of the block until I went inside. I realized that he'd been there for me all along.

Caregiving can be a gift in disguise—an experience that moves you toward a more meaningful connection with yourself and with others.

"And so I could hold him and say, 'I'm not giving you anything you didn't give to me, old man. I'm paying you back.' And I held him until he died. I didn't let go and I didn't let anyone else get in the way of that, either. I thought, 'I'm not letting go of this angel until he's gone.'"

Is it trite to repeat that old phrase, "Every ending offers a new beginning?" I don't think so. There are sound and sensible insights in each story I've collected that offer hope and understanding, and can nurture recovery and growth. Those I've spoken with often used the expression "the rewards of caregiving" to describe their experiences. Some have actually called their personal growth a transformation; others make reference to the gifts of caregiving. Often these gifts aren't perceived or understood until after the immediate pressures and concerns of active caregiving are past. This learning has no particular time frame. Yet, sometime during our lifetime, whether we're the caregiver or the recipient of care, there will be an opportunity to explore the possibilities of transforming hardship into hope, and to discover the incredible rewards and unexpected gifts of caregiving.

As you read the extraordinary stories of hardship, hope, and healing in this collection, I hope you will see that care-giving can be a gift in disguise—an experience that moves you toward a more meaningful connection with yourself and with others and a chance to nurture your spirit and trans-form your life.

The death of his young wife, Ellen, profoundly changed Allen's life. Despite the fear, grief, and depression caused by Ellen's illness and suffering, Allen was led in the unexpected direction of laughter and humor. For several years now, Allen has called himself "the world's only jolly-ologist." In his speeches around the country and in the books he's written, he shows people how to use hope and humor to deal with the not-so-funny stuff: illness, caregiving, loss, depression, and grief. We sat and talked together in the living room of his charming San Francisco home.

Ellen died here in our house. I brought her home from the hospital at around noon, then went out to buy food. When I came back, Ellen's mother ran out and said, "I think Ellen has died." Ellen was on the floor. She had fallen out of bed. I put a pillow under her head and held her hand. Ellen's mother was frightened. She didn't know what to do. Should she call the undertaker? I said no. When our

daughter came home from school, we all sat with Ellen quietly for a while, and then we called the funeral director. In the
hospital the body is removed immediately. This is awful for
the family and the primary caregivers. They need some time.
So we took the time we needed to say good-bye to Ellen.

But that's the end of my caregiving story. Here's the beginning. We had just married and were living in New York City
where I was freelancing as a scenic designer. We lived in an old
tenement, and the landlord was trying to get us out. Only
Ellen and I and one other tenant were left. One night there
was a mysterious fire. It was scary, but no one was hurt. The
next morning, the landlord gave us a big lump of money and
said we should leave. I'd always wanted to live in San
Francisco; it was my dream. I
didn't have a job waiting, but we
just packed and left New York.

In the hospital, the body is removed immediately. This is awful for the family and the primary caregivers. They need some time.

We moved on a Thursday,
and on Friday I went to the San
Francisco Opera, told them I
was a scenic designer, and asked
if they needed help. They told
me they were desperate for what I could offer, and I started
working the following Monday. We found this wonderful
Victorian house that we're sitting in now. I had always wanted to live in one and Ellen had, too. I remember that I used
to sit and draw pictures of Victorian houses when we were
living in New York. We had been in San Francisco about a
year when Ellen went for a check-up, and the doctor said
something was wrong. They did some blood tests, and it
turned out to be a rare liver disease. There was no cure. At
that time in 1975, only five liver transplants had been done.
The doctor said Ellen would live three years and, indeed, she
died in 1978.

Ellen was gregarious and fun, and had tons of friends.
She always wanted to party. The doctor said she should be in

bed, and Ellen said, "No, I'm going out dancing." She said she wanted to enjoy life. I would be upset that she wasn't taking care of herself, but she was determined to have fun. Once Ellen went into the bathroom and yelled that she was going to flush all her medications down the toilet. She was yelling, "Go down. Get out of here!"and laughing. I failed to see the humor. I couldn't laugh. Ellen was ill for three years. She had several operations; it was tough.

It was a very difficult time for us. I felt like there was nowhere to turn, no one to talk to. I went to a therapist, and he told me after the second session, "Life is difficult." I felt some anger toward him for this trite and unhelpful remark. Neither the therapist nor the doctor gave us any hope. I desperately needed hope. Somehow, even though you know the person won't make it, hope gets you through day to day. As Ellen became more ill and her friends knew she was dying, I could count on one hand the number of people who came around to visit her. She was

> *Somehow, even though you know the person won't make it, hope gets you through day to day.*

only thirty-one, and death frightened her peers, so a lot of them disappeared. Ellen was thin and yellow, and they didn't want to see her like that. Her friends only wanted to see the funny, outgoing Ellen.

When we were living in New York, a lot of our friends were separating and divorcing, and Ellen and I would ask each other, "Why are we still married?" Ellen would say, "You make me laugh." And that was one of the wonderful things about our relationship. We laughed a lot. It was one of the glues that held us together. But now I couldn't laugh.

Then one day, while I was visiting Ellen in the hospital, she handed me the centerfold from the latest *Playgirl* magazine and asked me to put it up on the wall. I said, "Ellen, I can't do that—this is a hospital." And she said,

"Okay, then get a big leaf off the plant over there and cover up 'that part.'" So I did, and it was fine for the first and second days, but by the third day the leaf had shriveled up, and what we had tried to hide was showing. We both laughed. It was only five or ten seconds of laughter, but it helped me get another perspective.

This was the beginning of how a scenic designer became what I call a "jolly-ologist." It gradually became clear to me that most caregivers don't see the humor even when it is there. I now give talks and facilitate workshops at hospitals, nursing homes, churches, and other organizations on the value of humor in the midst of illness, suffering, and death. Most of the time when I give my talks, I come onstage with a red clown nose either on my face or in my pocket. The groups I address are quite different from one another. I try to judge at what point in my performance the nose gimmick would best work to relax and engage each specific audience. When the event is over, I stand by the door to talk with those who want to exchange comments or stories, and I give everyone a red clown nose of their own.

Most caregivers don't see the humor even when it is there.

Once, my daughter encouraged a friend of hers, a rather depressed young man, to come to my talk. I spotted him reclining shyly at the rear of the room. As he left the room, he hastily grabbed a clown nose from my hand while I was in engaged in conversation. Many months later, my daughter told me that her friend, feeling deserted and hopeless, had been contemplating suicide. He told her how late one night as he stood in front of the bathroom medicine chest, he reached into his pocket and pulled out the clown nose. Without thinking, he put it on his face and saw his reflection in the mirror. "Tell your father that his clown nose may have saved my life," he later told my daughter. Seeing himself looking silly brought a spontaneous laugh. The deep gloom he had been feeling lifted just enough to cause him to change his plan. The stories I tell often lighten some very dark situations.

My father-in-law developed brain cancer and was hospitalized several times. For his and my mother-in-law's wedding anniversary, I suggested we have a small dinner party. I'd make a turkey and whatever else they wanted to serve and bring it over. My father-in-law was enjoying the meal, but he was starting to doze off at the table. He didn't hear very well so my mother-in-law passed him a note. She laughed as he read it, and he laughed, too. She had written, "Happy Anniversary, dear. Do you want to go to bed?" He very lovingly and quietly leaned over and said to her, "I'd love to, dear, but we have company."

Death and dying are not funny, but funny things do go on even when there is death and dying. When my dad passed away several years ago, my brother and I flew to Florida to sit Shiva with my mom. As I walked into my parents' home, I heard Mom on the phone with the rabbi, telling him that her sons were there with her. But she got tongue-tied and said, "My other son is going back to Connecticut to shit siver." We all broke into laughter. We howled so much that she couldn't talk and had to hand me the phone. I pulled myself together enough to tell the rabbi that we'd call him back.

Death and dying are not funny, but funny things do go on even when there is death and dying.

When I was taking care of Ellen, I often wished that a friend would come around to take me to a funny movie or play where I could laugh a little. Now I understand that caregivers need to find a bit of humor, some brief time out from the constant pressure and stress. Toward the end of Ellen's life I was running out of steam. Everything I did was for Ellen or my daughter. I didn't take very good care of myself. And I didn't understand that a good laugh could relieve stress or that a humorous perspective could lighten my burden. Many people have told me stories of laughter in the midst of loss, and I'm convinced that some higher power puts in some humor along with the hardship to help us through.

This understanding has had a profound influence on my life; it changed my career. To think that I'd get up in front of 1,500 family caregivers or professionals dealing with sickness and death and get them to laugh! I practically failed speech in college. But I realized I had a message about humor and loss, and every time I get up to speak it's a personal healing. There's always humor all around us. When we're caregivers we may not see it, but it is there. We need to stop for a moment and see it. And often caregivers are so busy they cannot take a moment. I realize when you're deeply involved in caregiving for a loved one it's like you're wearing blinders. My challenge is to show people there is humor and hope.

The greatest lesson I learned from my caregiving experience was to be, just to be, with Ellen. So many people think they have to do something. You don't have to do anything but sit with your loved one. I learned from being with Ellen how to be with others. If sadness came up, we cried; if humor happened, we laughed.

I'm a better person for having gone through caregiving. Those who have not yet experienced being around someone who is dying may not know that it makes you realize just how fragile life is. Every moment is precious. These valuable lessons are waiting to be learned, and you can smile, even laugh, while you're learning them.

ARDITH ECKARDT

In my travels, I've met many people who could be considered "long-distance caregivers"—daughters, sons, grandchildren, nieces, cousins, in-laws, relatives of all varieties who manage to care for a loved one from a distance. The responsibility often includes travel to distant locations, from a weekend trip to an extended stretch of time—whatever it takes to supervise and coordinate care. Each situation is managed differently, and every circumstance requires unique compromises. "You do what you feel you must do," Ardith told me when we talked about her mother and father. I arrived for my scheduled appointment with her on a Friday afternoon. Her car was packed for her regular weekend trip to see her parents. When we finished our conversation, she drove away before I even got into my car. She had a much longer drive to her destination than I did.

My parents live in a very small town on the South Dakota border about two hundred miles from the city where I live. They used to be farmers, and until recently they lived in their own home in the country. My mother is ninety-two. She suffers from dementia. My father is ninety. His mind is still very sharp, but he has major physical limitations. He fell a couple of years ago and severely injured himself. He can't walk, he's incontinent, and he has very little energy. When it became difficult to find help to come to their home and to get them the kind of nursing and personal services they needed, my four siblings and I thought it would be best for our parents to move into a nursing home. That's where they are now. I drive two hundred miles every weekend to visit them.

I just fell into the whole caregiving thing. I've always felt close to my parents, and caregiving seemed the right thing for me to do.

I guess you'd call me the primary caregiver. How did that happen when I have four brothers and sisters? Two of my siblings say they are too busy with their jobs and families to make the time; the other two have told me that it's just too hard for them to deal with the situation emotionally or to travel on a regular schedule. My sisters do come visit, but not as regularly as I do. I guess the dynamics of every family are different. I just fell into the whole caregiving thing. I've always felt close to my parents, and caregiving seemed the right thing for me to do. It's become a part of my lifestyle.

I began to go see my parents every weekend before they went to live in the nursing home. I could see how valuable my efforts were to them. I would drive up on the weekend after work and stay with them until Sunday night. I'd do the cleaning and the shopping and whatever was necessary to take care of them. I worked on making their house more wheelchair accessible. I installed a shower, built a deck, and tried to keep them comfortable in their home for as long as possible. Now I supervise their care in the nursing home, taking care of their financial matters as well as the house. They no longer live in it, but I bring my mother out to the house every weekend. My dad is in a wheelchair and needs a van to transport him. The local service isn't always available, but when it is he comes out to the house, too. He seems so tired; I think he's just shutting down. He's outlived his friends and everyone in his family. I know my mother is a real worry to him.

My mother loves flowers and is a dedicated gardener, so it gives her pleasure to be at her home. It's my responsibility to keep up the garden so she'll have flowers to pick. Because she has a fear of falling, we plant pots on the deck so she can enjoy flowers without going down the hill. And she likes to do things in the kitchen. She likes to wash the dishes after I've been cooking. These are things she can't do in the nursing home—familiar tasks that she's been doing all her life. Even though she's senile, she can still do these kinds of things. My mother doesn't eat because she's hungry; she eats for social reasons. So I take her to a restaurant or to my aunt's house, or we use her favorite dishes and cups and set the table with linens to make a social environment at home. I feel these are important things to do for her.

My mother doesn't eat because she's hungry; she eats for social reasons. So I take her to a restaurant or to my aunt's house, or we use her favorite dishes and cups and set the table with linens to make a social environment at home. I feel these are important things to do for her.

My mother is difficult; she has her ups and downs, and she's impatient about many things and demanding at times. I keep learning how to handle it—things are constantly changing, of course. I'm pretty familiar with her behavior, and when she can't find the words I can pretty much tell what she's trying to communicate. I've come to understand that certain things are disturbing to people who are losing their ability to communicate. For example, sometimes a nurse or an attendant will come into my parents' room in the nursing home with three people—one handing her medication, one combing her hair, and another cleaning the room. It's just too much for her, and she gets very agitated. Mother doesn't hear very well, but even if she hears she can't always make sense of what everyone is saying, and then she's uncooperative and you've lost her for a while. She knows that I'm one of her children, but she doesn't know exactly who I am, and she's beginning to confuse generations.

I know that the schedule I've taken on to care for my parents would put a terrible stress on most marriages. But my husband and I have become closer, and we understand one another better.

My coming every weekend is a help to my father as well. Although it's too hard for him to come with us to the house, it's a relief for him to know I'll be there every weekend to take care of my mother. And then, too, he knows the bills will be paid, the property will be taken care of, and nothing will be neglected. I've driven through snowstorms, rainstorms, and all kinds of weather to get there, and I've never let them down.

I know that the schedule I've taken on to care for my parents would put a terrible stress on most marriages. But my husband and I have become closer, and we understand one another better. My husband has been extremely supportive. I think he really admires what I'm doing. Sometimes he comes with me, but it isn't always convenient for him. We joke that having a few days apart is good for our relationship.

There's great joy for me in bringing some happiness to my folks and to the other older people at the nursing home. I've struck up relationships with some of the other residents in the nursing home. We've become friends, and sometimes I even take one or two of them on an outing. I don't think the administration at the nursing home particularly likes it when I take people other than my mom out to lunch. I'm sure I'm breaking some of their rules, but you know what? I'm glad I have the courage to break some of those rules to make one day better for people who might live the rest of their lives in the nursing home. To give them some pleasure, to make them smile, to hear them laugh, is so rewarding. I joke with one old farmer and always blame him for the weather. I bring in tractor books for some of the older men who were farmers all their lives. It's really easy to make some of these older people glow! This isn't just about my giving my time and effort to others. I really get a lot of satisfaction and pleasure back.

Once I was talking with a little old lady about birds or something, and pretty soon another lady came over and joined in the conversation. Nearby was another woman *This isn't just about my giving my time and effort to others. I really get a lot of satisfaction and pleasure back.* just sitting in her wheelchair, totally motionless, stiff and unresponsive. As the three of us talked, I noticed this woman's wheelchair backing up, and before I knew it she was sitting in our circle listening to the conversation. I'm finding that this happens a lot. The people in the nursing home need that social connection; when we all get to talking, they won't let me go!

I'd consider moving into my parent's house and living there except for my job. I work for a publisher and book distributor, and I love my job. I love books and my mother also cares a lot about books. It's the one thing she remembers. When I tell her on Sunday night that I'm leaving so I can go to work on Monday morning, she says, "Oh, what do you do? You work with books? Oh, how nice, that's nice work.

You are so lucky to work with books." She worked in the local library for years, and she was an avid reader. Those things she remembers.

I've learned a lot about giving care, and I've also learned something about myself. A few days with my parents, and I'm ready to get back to my own life until the next weekend. I can do caregiving well and I really enjoy it, but I need to take care of myself. Becoming a successful caregiver is a process of understanding your limitations.

Caregiving is probably the most rewarding thing I've ever done and also the most difficult. I know my mother probably doesn't remember the details of my visits, but I have the warm and wonderful experience of seeing her light up for that one minute when I arrive on the weekends. I think that the smiles and laughs we share keep her healthier. Sometimes she responds to me in such a way that you'd never know she was senile. I'll say to her, "You know, you're my best mom," and she'll reply, "That's because I'm your only mom!" She smiles every time we have that exchange. It's the best feeling for me. It makes my day.

BARB TILSEN

*"Your new book is about family caregivers?" my friend
Barb asked. "Come on over and we'll talk. I have some
stories to tell you," she volunteered. "Caregiving is
something we teach seriously and practice actively in my
family." When I arrived at Barb's house, she was sitting by
the fireplace in her living room, playing her guitar and
singing. "It's a new song, one I've just written. I'll sing the
whole thing for you later," she said.*

*Barb is a singer, songwriter, music educator, and
performer. I've heard her perform for both children and
adults. Barb specializes in events that mark life passages:
memorial services, funerals, bar mitzvahs, birth ceremonies.
In describing her career Barb says, "As a musician I see
myself as being a part of the kind of events that bring
families and communities together. As a teacher, an
educator, and artist, I try to capture personal memories
and special feelings." Now it was my turn to collect
personal memories and special feelings.*

My aunt Carol died two months ago at the age of eighty-eight. She had been in a nursing home for almost ten years, diagnosed with Alzheimer's. I was there on the day she died. She was agitated. I sat with her, held her hand, talked to her, and sang.

We take care of each other in our family. It's just how we function. For a long time, my mother took care of everyone in the family who was ill. She was always there for others. When my mother died three years ago, I felt I should take over for her as the primary caregiver. I knew that if she were still alive she'd be doing this for others in the family. I felt it was my responsibility to take over.

I sort of drifted into being the contact for Aunt Carol's care in the Alzheimer's unit she was living in. I went to her care conferences at the nursing home and kept in touch with her dietician, her physical therapist, and others responsible for her care. Aunt Carol's husband, my Uncle Bert, helped for a while. Then he became rather frail and needed help from the family as well. Six of us cousins in the younger generation formed a web of support around both Aunt Carol and Uncle Bert. My brother took charge of the main care for Uncle Bert—his bills as well as some personal care.

We take care of each other in our family. It's just how we function.

I recall how hard it was for Uncle Bert to put Aunt Carol in the nursing home. He wanted to be there with her all the time. They had been married for over sixty years, and their relationship was one of deep and abiding love.

When Uncle Bert's health started to fail, he moved into an assisted living situation. I would pick him up and take him to see Aunt Carol as often as I could. I sensed the deep connection between them, and I wanted to honor that. Spending time with Aunt Carol and Uncle Bert gave me the time and opportunity to observe a love story. When I brought Uncle Bert to visit with Aunt Carol, I'd walk away for a while so they could have their own time and space together. Although they were sitting together in wheelchairs in a room full of other people, I wanted them to have a feeling of privacy.

One day when I brought Uncle Bert to visit Aunt Carol she was in a grumpy, distant mood. Yet, after a short time I saw her reach out and touch his hand. Then she gently started stroking his hand and his arm. I watched as a soft, loving look came over her face. It brought tears to my eyes to watch them. It was incredibly beautiful for me to see that even if she might not have recognized him at first, she knew him by touch. They were truly connected. Observing this taught me a lot about love and about having a relationship that spans so much of your life and how deep that goes.

Being a caregiver has deepened the ways I think about love, family, and commitment. It hasn't been a burden for me. It's been a deep, personal journey— a very special experience.

My way of expressing my thoughts and feelings is to put them on paper and into music. My personal stories and experiences have become part of my performance repertoire. Inspired by Aunt Carol and Uncle Bert's lifelong relationship, I've written "Where Love Resides." Even when you read the words without the music, I think it speaks to the heart. I love to sing their story and share it with others.

"Can I sing it for you now?" Barb asked me. "Yes, of course," I replied. "I want to know more about where love resides and how, in spite of dementia, aging, and loss, it survives." Barb began to sing. The words came from her heart, from her deep love and compassion.

One single tear spills down my cheek.
I am struck,
thinking how tragic, how sad,
that after a lifetime of loving each other
it comes down to this:
sitting together,
side by side,
wheelchair to wheelchair,
holding hands.
That's all there is, nothing more.

I've brought him to see her again,
to the Oasis unit,
locked ward of the nursing home
for those on the steady downward slope
of Alzheimer's decline.
You can't get out the door unless you know the code,
can't get out of this disease at all.
No one knows that code.

We sit with sunlight streaming in the windows.
This big room is peaceful and calm today.
Other times, residents have wandered by
shouting or swearing,
"Take me home! Bring me back!"
"Where's my furniture? Where's my kitchen?"
"I want my mother."
But today is different.
This lounge is quiet, tranquil.
No one crying out, no moaning,
no loud voices talking to thin air,
to a long-gone lover or friend, daughter or son,
a forgotten argument in some long-ago time.
No one moving in that slow solo dance
within fragments of old memories.

We sit, with me on his left.
He is in the middle, she is on his right.
I am drifting in memories myself,
of childhood gatherings, laughter, and loving faces,
my grandma and my grandpa,
my mom and my dad,
who've all passed on now,
sweet memories alive, but only in my heart.
I think about this aunt and this uncle I sit with today,
both in their eighties, married almost sixty years.
She seems oblivious, very much inside herself.
Barely smiles when we first sit down,
staring ahead with a kind of sour look on her face.
Doesn't recognize me as her niece, or him as her husband.
Those days seem past
since she could look at him and call him by his name.

Long time since we've been able to sit
and talk about the same thing, or anything.
Even have a conversation grounded
in the same perceived present reality.
Sometimes she'll talk in half-formed sentences,
words strung together in ways
I can barely follow or understand,
fleeting memories bobbing in and out of a crazy quilt of time.
Another silent tear rolls down my cheek as I muse in the sunlight,
bittersweet—a lifetime of loving condensed
into a passing moment together.

He reaches out and takes her hand as he often does when we visit.
Sometimes she quietly holds his hand, too.
But today is different.
This day, as he holds her hand,
She slowly starts to squeeze his back.
Then she strokes it, and her face changes.

Smiling, she says, "Oh, oh, oh."
She touches his fingers, his thumb, and the back of his hand.
She says, "This is nice,"
as though her skin recognizes his.
Her mind can't say his name, but her body knows him,
memory and love living bone deep.
She touches his hand, his arm,
his shirt sleeve, and says again,
"This is nice!"
He says, "Oh yes, I like this shirt, it's a good shirt."
She sits back, her hand holding his,
her whole face transformed
with a gentle, sweet, contented smile.

It is amazing to be together in this rare moment,
sharing the same intersection of time and space.
One single tear spills down my cheek.
I am struck,
thinking how incredible,
how profoundly beautiful,
that, after a lifetime of loving each other,
it all comes down to this:
sitting together,
side by side,
wheelchair to wheelchair.
In their holding hands
the heart bridges the gap
the mind alone cannot leap
where touch knows touch,
skin knows skin,
and love resides cell-deep
weaving memory and connection.

My caregiving experience with Aunt Carol has profoundly affected my sense of parenting and the importance of family connection. I made sure that I often brought my children to visit Aunt Carol. I wanted them to see that we take care of each other and that the generations of family are connected in this way. Caring for Aunt Carol and Uncle Bert has taught us what it really means to be a family. Uncle Bert tells other people, "No one has great nieces and nephews like I have." But I tell him, "Uncle Bert, in letting us care for you and Aunt Carol, you taught us that." My grandparents, my parents—they all did it for each other, so it only feels natural that we should be doing this, too. Being a caregiver has deepened the ways I think about love, family, and commitment. It hasn't been a burden for me. It's been a deep, personal journey—a very special experience.

BILL AND JUDY THOMAS

It was winter, and there had been an enormous amount of snowfall in upstate New York. Flights to Syracuse were being canceled regularly, so I decided to take the bus to visit with Dr. Bill Thomas and his wife, Judy. They live outside Sherburne, New York, with their five children. We talked about their work before we talked about the children. Several years ago, Bill Thomas started the Eden Alternative movement that has humanized hundreds of nursing homes throughout America. The changes have come through bringing plants, pets, and children into nursing homes and other living situations that previously lacked an atmosphere of homelike warmth.

On their property, adjacent to where they live, they've recently built a modest-sized, inviting retreat center where they host weekend seminars designed to explore ways of creating positive change in our society. "It's a place for intelligent and passionate discussion that plants seeds for change," according to Judy and Bill Thomas.

*We sat at their kitchen table after dinner. Zachary, age
twelve, and Virgil, age ten, were in the living room doing
whatever young boys do to avoid paying attention to their
homework. Caleb, the baby of the family, was already in
bed for the night. Their daughter Haleigh, age six, was
being fed strained baby food by a nurse; their other
daughter Hannah, age four, was lying in a special reclining
stroller. The girls were exceptionally small, each weighing
around thirty pounds. Both were born with Otahara
syndrome, a malfunctioning of the nerve cells. Both are
blind, suffer from seizures, are susceptible to respiratory
infections, and require continuous nursing care.*

*You might expect the Thomas home to resemble a
hospital or clinic, but you'd be mistaken. Their place has
the warmth and charm of a country farmhouse. The room
where Haleigh and Hannah sleep has a specially designed
and crafted bed that is an elegant piece of furniture with
sides that come up to prevent the girls from falling out. An
adjacent bathroom has been designed to accommodate the
assistance of a nurse for all bathing and toilet functions.
Their room is warm and cozy, decorated with dolls and
other toys, although Hannah and Haleigh will never be
able to play with them.*

*Everything visible reflects the normal appearance of a
young girl's room. Yet, this is not a "normal" situation.
Judy served tea, and the three of us sat together watching
the snow fall outside through the large window. It was time
for conversation. I listened while they told of their
heartaches and their joys. Judy was the first to speak.*

B oth of our little girls have Otahara syndrome. This
disease is so rare that there are only thirty known diagnosed cases in the world. It took about six weeks
before we realized there was something wrong. Then we were
told that there was no cure. They told us Haleigh would not

live six months. The doctors told us it wasn't genetic and that we could have another child. And then Hannah was born, and within twenty-four hours she had a seizure and we were headed down the same path. It's an issue with my eggs. We have two older boys. They're my stepsons, so they're well. Sometimes I look at the girls and think it's all my fault. It hurts. I struggle. We chose to have an egg donor for our last child.

The girls live with us and are part of the family. We made the decision that we weren't going run around to doctors looking for miracles, so we just brought them home. People say we are such special people to do this. We're not. You do what you have to do.

Having the girls has made me realize that I'm a lot stronger than I ever thought I could be. If

People say we are such special people to do this. We're not. You do what you have to do.

you had told me when I was in my twenties that I'd have two children like this and I could live with it, I would have thought you were crazy. But you handle it; you get up in the morning and you just do it.

When Haleigh was born, I was devastated. When I found out she wasn't neurologically normal, I didn't know what that meant. Once I understood, I withdrew from the baby and didn't want to touch or hold her. I chose to disconnect because I was told she wouldn't live past six months. And then something changed, and I scooped her into my arms and knew I'd love her. I still feel horrible about this. What a time!

The most important lesson for me was to mourn the two children I didn't have. Before you can accept what you get, you need to mourn the loss of your expectations. When I'd see a child the same age, I'd cry. And then there was anger; you know the steps. Yet, eventually, I let go of what I thought would be a normal life with a normal child.

My girls can't talk or see. They can hear music, they can

smile and react. And they can show us when they are sad. That's the hardest thing for me because they can't tell us why. That hurts. I wish they could talk. But we just try one thing and another, and eventually something works.

We didn't want our home to look like a hospital. We have the things we might need, like oxygen and other medical equipment. But we've made a special bed for the girls to look nicer than hospital furniture, and a special bathroom and shower. Sure, you can tell they're disabled and have special needs, but our home doesn't look like it's set up like that. You might say that we run a long-term care service in our home.

We have round-the-clock nurses. Our nurses are exceptional; they're an extension of our home and our family. They share both our joys and our sorrows. We really want our daughters to be with us, to be part of our family. They used to call children such as our girls "throw-away babies." They'd go to an institution, without a being given a name, without being given the care they need-

The most important lesson for me was to mourn the two children I didn't have. Before you can accept what you get you need to mourn the loss of your expectations.

ed—and they'd perish. One of our nurses said to me one day, "Your girls are alive because of the love you give them." I believe that's true. Our love, the love of our other children, and our nurses' love make all the difference in our world, and theirs.

This is the kind of thing you've got to deal with directly. There's no way of hiding or covering it up. Our marriage was challenged, but we're strong now, and so solid. A friend of ours had a disabled child around the same time Haleigh was born. The baby died, and, sadly, the marriage was ruined. I really don't know our secret. But I do know that something like this can actually make a marriage and a family stronger.

Then Bill joined the conversation.

Our biggest fear is that we will run out of funding for nursing care. But we'll figure it out because we'd never put the girls into an institution. We see that they have a life of peace and joy and tenderness. There is joy to be found and love to be felt no matter what they can or can't do. I spend a lot of time speaking to nurses and doctors about caregiving. Even if I don't specifically mention my girls, what I say is informed by my experience at home. It has made me a better teacher and physician.

The two older boys don't realize they're having a very rare childhood experience, unlike any other. Just last Saturday they had friends come over to play, and my boys just said to their friends casually, "That's Haleigh and that's my sister Hannah," and then they zoomed onto the next thing they were doing. Once they went to a public playground, and my younger son saw that the handicapped swing was far removed from all the others, and he asked why they would do such a thing. They're growing up without a sense of shame or remorse about the life that they live. Our boys are more accepting of others' differences, and that's carried over to all kinds of people. That's a real gift of learning. I actually think they're growing up wiser souls.

> *One of the cruel truths of caregiving in America is that we have reduced the idea of caregiving to providing medication, therapy, and exercises. This is part of the story, but it's not the whole story.*

Our daughters survive with the help of a lot of potent medications, but we deliver them in the context of love. One of the cruel truths of caregiving in America is that we have reduced the idea of caregiving to providing medication, therapy, and exercises. This is part of the story, and we can't deny the value of medications, but it's not the whole story.

Here's a little irony. Let's say you are taking care of someone, and you pour out your heart and soul and give your love and tenderness. Let's say they get better. One of the first things that happens is that the financing service, the insurance company or whomever, will kick the ladder out from under you. The system came back to us and said, "Look, your girls haven't had to be hospitalized for a time now. They're okay, right?" And we say, "That's because the financial help allows us to get good nursing. That's how we've kept them out of the hospital." Nevertheless, they remove the supports that have allowed things to get better and take away one of the key elements of success, making it much harder to continue the care. It's hard convincing anyone unless you've lived this. Yet, it's more than a personal problem; it's a political problem in American society.

We're blessed that we live in a time when there are home-based alternatives, but accessing that home care means engaging in a running battle with the bureaucracy.

At this point in our conversation, Bill had to leave. Judy and I continued to talk.

Bill and I have made a commitment to end the plague of how the elderly in our society are institutionalized. There are approximately eight million people who go to sleep, or don't go to sleep, in a nursing home every night. We're dedicated to changing the character of the way the frail and elderly are cared for. At the same time, we're faced with how to take care of very ill, very fragile children. In the past, they would have been placed in an institution. We're blessed that we live in a time when there are home-based alternatives, but accessing that home care means engaging in a running battle with the bureaucracy. We're engaged in fighting bureaucratic structures on both fronts.

We really want to see change in our society. I want people to start looking at and revering our elders, and looking at and accepting people with disabilities and children who are different from other children—and stop turning away. People will say how beautiful one of our "normal" children is and will just pass over the girls and look the other way.

Our work and our teaching is about understanding how important it is that a society provides for and organizes itself to meet the needs of the frail and disabled in the most humane way, so we have a better society for everybody. Our calling is to create a more engaging, more forgiving, more caring, and warmer culture. Caregiving for our girls has taught us a lot about this. Maybe we can teach others about making a place that is just and equitable and mindful of the needs of the elderly and the disabled, and everyone will benefit. You don't need to be a family caregiver to understand these needs, but we've learned a lot from our personal experiences.

Nobody comes into a caregiving or care-receiving situation on a voluntary basis. The truth is, we come to it kicking and screaming. All of us.

Nobody comes into a caregiving or care-receiving situation on a voluntary basis. The truth is, we come to it kicking and screaming. All of us. What we now have in our own home is a microcosm of how we'd like the world to work. Of course, there are many people in the world who don't have to think about these things right now, but it seems that everybody gets to some version of where we are sooner or later. Look around. It touches everybody. Family caregiving issues are something everyone everywhere in some way will have to deal with.

Our home is the absolute center of our universe. Caregiving for Haleigh and Hannah has put the focus of our work here at home. A huge part of what allows us to do our work professionally is that we live it every day. Everyday life teaches us, and then we teach others from our hearts, from our experience; our girls come into our teaching always.

You asked us what we've learned from our personal caregiving experience. Well, we've certainly learned about the importance of living one day at a time. And our experience has shown us what a strong marriage we have. You learn little things every day—not always astronomical stuff, but the awareness of small things: the joy of going out for a walk, the pleasure of seeing how the trees look covered with snow.

And then there's the big stuff, the constant and unremitting reminder that you love your children just the way they are. There's joy to be found and love to be felt no matter what. We're thankful for everything that we have. And maybe the girls are thankful, too, in their way, for lives that are filled with peace, joy, and tenderness. They suffer some physical pain, and that's hard to watch. We struggle with this because you always hear that God never gives you more than you can handle. But why us? Why them? It was hard to accept. But they are loved and they know that, and the rest falls into place.

There's a lot of love here, and that's the gift.

CAROL SEGRAVE

Divorced, with two grown children, Carol Segrave was living alone, building an interesting and rewarding consulting career while enjoying an active social life. Except for her concern for her eighty-year-old mother, things were just fine. Like many children of aging parents, Carol lived far away from her mother. Three thousand miles separated Carol from an aging and fragile mother who lived alone and refused to have any help in the house.

For as long as Carol could remember, her mother, who had been widowed for over fifty years, had been an incredibly strong, independent woman. But now the old family home was in bad need of repair. Carol monitored her mother's health and daily activity as diligently as the distance and commitments to her job and personal life allowed.

Carol flew from California to New Jersey six or seven times a year, bought two months worth of groceries at a time, filled the freezer, cleaned the house, and organized her mother's affairs as best she could. Then she'd fly home and phone her mom four or five times a day to be sure she was okay. Carol watched her mom slowly deteriorate yet remain determined to stay in her own home, no matter what.

When I interviewed Carol, she was fifty-two. A year had passed since the death of her mother, Alice. Carol and I sat together drinking tea and looking back at her caregiving experience. She shared the story of how she had decided to handle it, and all she had learned.

It was stressful, I'll tell you. One summer I went back to New Jersey with a plan to spend the summer with Mother. I thought that I'd certainly be coming back to California in the fall, but I had to face the reality that she was getting weaker and weaker. I came to the conclusion that it was better for me to put my life in California temporarily on hold and go stay with her. I knew I could no longer deal

I realized I couldn't cure Mother, but I could work on healing myself.

with the stress and frustration of being a long-distance caregiver. I finished up my consulting contracts, gave notice on the house I was renting, put virtually everything I owned in storage, packed up what I needed, and moved across the country and into her house.

At first, I felt alone and missed the life I had left behind. But gradually I began to take hold of my new situation. I found the neighbors to be some of the dearest, sweetest, finest people I'd ever met—the salt of the earth. They were incredibly supportive of me during the last eighteen months of my mother's life. And I reconnected with cousins, my last remaining uncle, and other members of my family—a bonus I hadn't counted on. I felt love and support from each neighbor, relative, and old friend. It was truly a beautiful and unexpected experience.

I realized that I couldn't cure Mother, but I could work on healing myself. There I was, sleeping in the bed I slept in when I was eight years old, preparing meals on the stove I learned to cook on when I was ten. I spent time walking the streets of the town I grew up in, past the homes where relatives and friends once lived, past the church I was married in and the school where I went from kindergarten through the tenth grade. It became a time for healing a lot of the issues related to the death of my father when I was very young. I was dealing with feelings of sadness and grief that I never imagined I would revisit, much less resolve and heal.

My relationship with my mother had always been good. But we became deeply, deeply close. Over those eighteen months of caregiving, I learned so much about the death and dying. It was a powerful, intense, in-the-trenches education in caregiving—the psychological side of it, the spiritual side of it, the physical side of it—bathing her, cleaning her, looking for miracles, putting everything I had into trying to keep her alive.

You just can't do it alone. I learned this quickly. Everyone needs some measure of help, of respite, in these situations.

I don't remember the hard parts. It might sound strange, but I only remember the good stuff. I remember how wonderful it was to slow down and just sit on snowy afternoons and listen to her. I remember going out to dinner with friends and coming home at midnight, and finding her sitting on the sofa at age eighty-nine just the way she did when I was nineteen years old, saying to me, "I was so worried about you. How can you do this to me? How can you make me worry about you?" It was really adorable to have my mom still care that much. Other people might freak out and say, "Mom, I'm over fifty years old!" But I was deeply touched, because I knew that soon she wouldn't be sitting on that sofa anymore. Those final years when people are slipping away from us are so precious.

My mother was fading, but at least I didn't have the stress of dealing with someone who was dying of cancer or in constant pain. When she experienced her last bout of congestive heart failure, I took her to the hospital and she slipped into a coma. I said to the doctor, "What's happening here?" The doctor said, "She'll linger like this for five or six days. There's nothing more we can do." And I said, "I want to take her home to die where she'd want to be."

My mom was blessed to have had a wonderful companion caregiver who helped me care for her those last few months. You just can't do it alone. You've got to have a helpmate in this process. I learned this quickly. Everyone needs some measure of help, of respite, in these situations. The two of us brought her home and put her in her bed of sixty-seven years and brushed her hair and put on the prettiest nightgown we could find; then we sat with her for three days and held her hand. And one night she just stopped breathing.

So it was eighteen months of caregiving, laughing, crying, hugging, sharing, going over photographs, celebrating holidays, arguing, and being impatient with each other. I was terrified as she declined physically, but somehow I found the strength and the courage to—to let her go. Looking back on those months, I feel it's important to tell you what I learned. Caring for my mother helped me face something I had managed to avoid before: thinking about death, about mortality, about how fragile we humans are. We're only here for a little while. We need to let those around us know that we love them, that we care about them, that they matter to us. I pay attention to this now. I let my family and friends know that I care about them, that they're important in my life. Through taking care of my dying mother, I learned as much about living life as about facing death.

CLIFF SAGER

It was a good time in their lives. Their children were grown, the busy years of building a career were over. It was time to travel, explore new interests and hobbies, and enjoy life. Cliff was a therapist who saw clients in his office adjacent to their spacious suburban home. Cathy was active, friendly, and well liked. We had become friends, and I looked forward to our times together. Her conversation was informed, thoughtful, bright, and witty. It was fun to be with her.

One day Cathy discovered a small lump in her breast. She went to the doctor immediately; although he was reassuring, the doctor suggested it might be wise to have a biopsy. This story is not about recovery from cancer but about a beautiful relationship that grew deeper as Cathy's illness progressed. Cliff talked with me about the woman he loved and lost.

I remember very clearly the day Cathy came into my office and told me the results of the biopsy. She had breast cancer. Everything followed from that—surgery, decisions about chemotherapy, a follow-up that revealed another lump, more surgery, more chemotherapy. It seemed endless.

Through it all, I came to understand at a profound level that it was vital to find ways to deal with things. I learned a new appreciation for ways of coping that are often described as denial. You need to develop certain frames of mind in order to deal with serious illness. You must find ways of surviving, of holding together, dealing with what comes next, taking care of yourself, and being helpful to and supportive of the person you're caring for. It's not just what people blithely refer to as "defenses." It's how people survive; it's how I survived.

I think we were realistic about the severity of Cathy's illness, but we also knew we had to have hope. The one thing that was hopeful for me was uncertainty. All through my wife's illness, even when her illness recurred after a period of remission, I still clung to the hope that perhaps, statistically, she would be in the most fortunate category. I guess what happens is that gradually the circle of hope narrows and narrows. For us, it was during the summer of the year she would die that we both really knew there weren't many options left.

You need to develop certain frames of mind in order to deal with serious illness. You must find ways of surviving, holding together, dealing with what comes next, taking care of yourself, and being helpful to and supportive of the person you're caring for.

It was the end of the season, and we were closing up our summer vacation home. Usually we closed it up with the anticipation of returning the following spring. But this time we both knew that was not going to happen. I remember the last day we walked on the beach together. We were aware that this was the last time we'd take this walk together. It was a terribly sad day. It was the first of many times through this whole process that we knew it was the last time we'd share something together.

We were about to leave the beach, and both Cathy and I were on the edge of weeping when we bumped into some neighbors who were chattering away. It was like a scene out of a movie; those people talking and talking at a moment that was for us so poignant and painful. Paradoxically, it somehow helped us. I didn't know how we were going to leave the beach that day. It was a place of so many memories, so many summers together, so many times walking together, picking up seashells, playing with our children, and sharing our lives. It was terribly painful, yet we had to face it and we didn't quite know how. Somehow this chattering couple enabled us to get through it. I saw it as a kind of a blessing. I think we would have just collapsed otherwise.

The treatment had become the illness; it had become worse than the disease.

That fall we knew Cathy was approaching the end. The oncologist told us about another new drug they were testing and suggested we consider more chemotherapy. It was then that, together, we consciously chose a different path. We had gone through enough. The treatment had become the illness; it had become worse than the disease. We decided that Cathy would not have any further treatments, and that had a very positive effect. It was sad, but we felt somehow that we were in control and her illness was no longer living us. We knew now that whatever time was left, we would have it together.

We became as close as two human beings could possibly become. When I look back, it was a time that I really cherish. I'm so grateful we had that together. We spent a lot of time reviewing our lives together—the good things, the joys, and the fullness of it all. We talked about everything. Cathy and I had a very good marriage, a wonderful marriage, but like all marriages it also had some rough spots. There were some mean, thoughtless things we had done or said to each other in the past, as couples often do. Now we had an opportunity to come to some peace about those things. We forgave each other for some of the rough times we had given one another. It was very important that we had the time and the wisdom to do this.

And there was something else that we talked about. Cathy told me she wanted me to marry again. Part of me felt guilty about even thinking of remarrying. It seemed like a betrayal. But I knew she was being honest. Cathy didn't want my loneliness and suffering to be her legacy. I sincerely believe she wanted me to remarry. I felt I had her blessing. It was to honor her spirit that I did go on with my life and eventually did marry again.

Of course, a large part of me still wishes Cathy was here in my life. Her death was an enormous blow to me. I was really wiped out for quite a while.

I've come to understand that the most important thing we possess is time.

Some of my friends who had also lost a spouse told me that you never really get over it, and I've found that to be true. You never get over missing someone who was important to you, and that knowledge sits side by side with the new relationship.

I feel very blessed that I eventually met a woman who was able to understand and accept that. It actually was a number of years later that Judith came into my life. I don't feel that she and Cathy are in competition with each other. They each have their place in my life. I can miss Cathy, and I certainly do, and still enjoy being with the woman to whom I'm married now. She and I are able to talk about that. It's been important in our marriage. I don't know how I could have managed a new relationship otherwise.

The experience of Cathy's illness and death has made me better able to be with other people who are experiencing pain.

In my work as a therapist, I'm much more available now to people who are suffering, in pain, or facing death. I know we can't always relieve pain and suffering, but we can be with other people, stay with them, be available to them, and not abandon them. I never realized how much I tended to withdraw from people in pain. We can't make some circumstances of life different, but we can stay with each other, support each other. I've learned to do this in a way that never would have been possible for me before. That's one of the ways I've changed and grown from the experience of Cathy's death.

Another significant thing I've learned through all of this is about time. Oh, I knew it intellectually, but now I know it in a fuller, more profound way. What I mean is I've come to understand that the most important thing we possess is time. I began learning that during Cathy's illness. We created more time for each other. I worked less, we spent more time alone together, we both learned to think about time in a different way, and I still do.

When you really know that your time will come to an end, when you're aware of death, I think you value time in a different way. It's the one thing you have control over, how you spend your time. This awareness has carried over into my life now. I continually ask myself, "Is this how I want to use the time that's left in my life?" I see clearly in what areas of my life I have control—and what things I can't control. I think of the phrase "living more fully," and that's what I do now. I learned from dealing with Cathy's illness and death how to live more consciously and with more awareness.

Cynthia grew up on a farm, the eldest of five. She's married, has two teenage children, and still lives on a farm. "I'm just an ordinary person," she told me when we talked, but I found her most extraordinary. She has worked as an interior designer, an acting coach, and a professional model, but her passion is to help and encourage others to be the best they can be in whatever field they choose. Her self-described mission is "to help you to recognize your individual gifts and tap into your creative energies so you can sparkle and soar in every area of your life." Her inspiration to give this to others came from her dad. She calls him her angel.

My dad was my hero. He was incredibly caring; he loved his wife and his children more than anything in the world. We were all stars in his eyes.

One day, my sister called me and said, "Oh Cynthia, Daddy is dying." She was hysterical. Dad had started throwing up blood; the doctor suspected a rare form of cancer, Leiomyosarcoma. My dad had no symptoms, except maybe heartburn. But we're Italian. We eat lots of spicy food. My father wasn't concerned about symptoms of indigestion. He had never been sick a day in his life. Now I was being told that the doctors have given him only three weeks to live.

I thought about all the times my dad had been there for me. I began calling every doctor I knew. I called around the country and found the most respected experts on this kind of cancer. I was absolutely shameless in asking for help. If the doctors were right and he only had a few weeks to live, I had to act fast. I kept hoping, even though I was told over and over again that a cancer that large could not be operated on and nothing could be done. Even if a cure wasn't possible, I thought maybe there was a way to get some time. I guess I really believe that miracles happen to those who believe in them, and I really believed.

My dad's last days truly were a gift. When he died, there were absolutely no regrets.

The first miracle was that I found a doctor who thought there was a chance with surgery. Then there was another miracle. The surgery gave my father a few more years of quality life. He went back to his ranch, planted a vineyard, installed an irrigation system, finished building a dam, and took a number of trips. Three years later, the cancer came back with ferocity. At this point, I realized we couldn't look toward a cure. The cancer had metastasized, and Daddy knew that he was dying. I told him I would be there with him until the very last breath. It was both the most difficult time and the most rewarding experience of my life.

My dad's last days truly were a gift. When he died, there were absolutely no regrets. Those three years that were supposed to be three weeks had given us the time to realize the beauty of life. We experienced deeply how much we really loved each other, and we didn't hesitate to say it. I came to understand during that time that we only have this moment. I was able to say to my dad, "You are a gift. I love you. Thank you for all you've done. You've made a difference in my life, you've made a difference in the community, and you've made a difference in the world just by your being."

In the final weeks, I stayed close to my dad and we talked a great deal. One day he smiled at me and said, "I'm dying a happy man. I married the woman I love and have shared forty-five years with her. I have five fabulous children, and I was blessed to be a farmer. It was my passion. I tilled the soil, and what I did fed people. I've lived my dream." What he said gave me a profound insight. This simple man, a salt-of-the-earth farmer, felt he had lived his destiny, his purpose, his dream. I thought, "Why are so many of us striving to be something we aren't in this world, struggling to fulfill someone else's idea of success, someone else's dream?" At that moment, my whole life changed. I realized that it was vitally important for each of us to truly be who we are, who we were born to be, to be the star we are—to find that light that shines within and help that light shine bright.

I realized that it was vitally important for each of us to truly be who we are, who we were born to be, to be the star we are—to find that light that shines within and help that light shine bright.

When my dad died his last words to me were, "My end is your beginning." It was true. Since then I've created and hosted a television program called *Be the Star You Are*. It's about people who are doing what they love, not for the money, not for the glamour, but because what they chose to do feeds their soul. I really didn't know anything about pro-ducing a television show, so it's nothing short of a miracle that I was able to find people who supported my efforts and helped me broadcast twenty-eight shows. For the most part, all of the people I interviewed on the program were ordinary people who had followed their passion and fulfilled their dream. There was very little money to do the show, but somehow I found volunteers to donate their time and energy. I actually paid my camera crew with vegetables from my garden and fresh chicken eggs! I didn't do this program for money; it was my gift of inspiration to others. I dedicated the series to my dad who had been my inspiration. I've recently written a book called *Be the Star You Are: 99 Gifts for Living, Loving, Laughing, and Learning to Make a Difference.* I wrote it with love. I want to inspire others, and I know now that I can do that.

I treasure those years of my dad's illness even as I remember how difficult they were. Being able to care for him and to help was such a joy because it was in that time that I learned the meaning of life. I learned that it doesn't matter how many medals you win, how many trophies you have, how much money you've made. There's only one thing at the end of the day and at the end of our lives that matters, and that is love—loving and respecting yourself and showing others that you care about them. Loving is how we really make a difference. My dad taught me that. He was my teacher, my angel, my hero.

DANA REEVE

Dana Reeve is the wife and primary caregiver for her husband, actor Christopher Reeve, who suffered a paralyzing spinal cord injury when he was thrown from his horse. Most of us remember him in the role of Superman. After you read this conversation with Dana Reeve, you might agree she deserves the label of Superwoman. I had an opportunity to meet and talk with her when I was producing my one-hour special for public radio entitled, "Hardship into Hope: The Rewards of Caregiving." Dana Reeve was most generous in discussing the changes and challenges and the profound learning that resulted from their situation. Our conversation took place a few years after her husband's accident. At the time, their son Will was six.

The accident instantly transformed life as our family knew it. Chris's life was changed; all of our lives were changed. His, of course, the most profoundly. He's the one that can't just hop out of bed. He's the one that can't even scratch an itch. Now, those are huge changes.

I was able to cope better than I ever would have believed. Family rushed in, friends rushed in, neighbors were incredible. There was an energy that came up for me; it was all about problem-solving. Day by day, it was about getting things done—taking care of the insurance, filling out forms, talking with doctors—and I told myself, as many other women I've spoken with, "I can do it, I can do it, I can do it. Whatever it is, I can do it, I can cope with it, I can do it all." It takes a tremendous amount of energy, almost manic energy.

There's that sobering realization that we have to endure not only what has already been endured, but we have to continue to live like this. This is now the status quo. This is normal life.

And then, about eighteen months into it, there is the settling and sinking realization and the slowing down where you realize, okay, this is not a sprint. This is a long distance jog, and I'd better settle into a rhythm. Then along with that comes a down period, for the caregiver and the recipient of the care as well. For Chris and myself, and for others in similar situations, there's that sobering realization that we have to endure not only what has already been endured, but we have to continue to live like this. This is now the status quo. This is normal life.

One of the things that I've realized is that I'm part of a group called "caregivers," and there are millions of us. Caregiving someday touches all our lives. Former First Lady Rosalynn Carter in her book about caregiving said something like, "It's going to touch all our lives. You either have been a caregiver, are going to be caring for someone, or you're going to need to be cared for." It's often something that we take on willingly because we love the person and because we feel it's our duty, and yet we don't see it as a job, necessarily, and it really is. Not that we wouldn't do it anyway.

I do realize that I'm in a position that many, many other people are not—a position of privilege. I'm able to have people help me out with things like housework. I'm able to have a babysitter. And I don't have to worry about how much that costs. We're not going to be forced to go on Medicare or Medicaid. We have twenty-four-hour nursing, but when that stops, as it will soon, we have other financial resources we can count on. So that removes a tremendous amount of stress that I just don't have to experience. Yet, I realize that many, many people have that stress.

For the first ten months, I was doing most of the physical care myself and training the staff we have now. Slowly I weaned myself from the physical care. My caregiving now is almost entirely emotional. The more difficult task, I find, is the emotional caregiving. I remember once reading an article, before Chris's injury, about a woman whose husband suffered chronic depression over a long period of time and about how difficult it was for her as his caregiver. And I remember I thought that surely she could get away from that or handle it some way, and I passed it off. I think of that now and realize how smug that response of mine was.

In many ways, dealing with a loved one's depression and negative emotions is more difficult than the physical care.

I know now that, in many ways, dealing with a loved one's depression and negative emotions is more difficult than the physical care. I can lift all day long. I can wipe a face or wipe a bottom. There's a beginning, a middle, and an end to those tasks. You do it, you've achieved it, and it's done. Dealing with someone's emotions is much more complicated, much more messy, much more ongoing. I've grown a lot in my understanding. I'm not so sure how to really describe it all. But the reality of the hardship of life is much more present. Life is about compromise and coping with difficulties. I'm doing some of that, and I think I've really grown.

I have never really plunged into despair. I have down moments, but I can honestly say they're not very frequent. Something that Chris often speaks about is, when he feels the most down and the most sorry for himself, he focuses on other people and what he can offer them. That helps him out of his funk. Chris helps a lot of young kids who've had spinal cord injuries. A lot of people who have spinal cord injuries, especially young men in their late teens and early twenties, talk with him about wanting to die. He knows how to deal with them and help them understand that compromise is going to be a way of life, that it feels lousy now but you're going to be okay and handle it. Chris has talked to a couple of kids and truly has saved their lives. He's been incredible that way. And what he does bolsters him.

When Chris feels the most down and the most sorry for himself, he focuses on other people and what he can offer them.

And I find the same thing for myself when I speak to groups (particularly to women who are caregivers) about strategies to survive difficulty. I find that it re-energizes me. I feel like I'm doing something worthy. I'm producing good out of bad; this thing has happened, and yet we've helped a tremendous number of people. I speak on the subject of nurturing the nurturer and how important it is for caregivers to do good things for themselves. Caregivers need to give themselves permission to do something self-indulgent, relaxing, and completely removed from their caregiver responsibilities. You need to find ways to sustain yourself for the long haul. The person needing care always has needs to be filled, whether they're emotional or physical. So caregivers must take time for themselves.

What Chris is able to give back to me is the same thing he's able to give to the world. He inspires me. There's something about being with somebody with a disability who, against all odds, achieves the goals he sets for himself, that can't help but be inspiring to those around him. You really don't feel like you can complain about your own problems, and, truly, you don't even feel like complaining when you see someone who is dealing with a life that's so difficult moment to moment and not only getting through it but doing so much for others.

I so admire how he handles his job as a parent, as a father. His job is doubly hard. Chris would love to be able to be out there coaching some of the sports that Will plays. But he goes to the games if the weather isn't too cold and cheers Will on. Chris loves hockey and would want to be able to be out there with him. He played hockey in high school and college. But he puts his feelings aside—it hurts him, I know—and he goes to support Will.

Caregivers need to give themselves permission to do something self-indulgent, relaxing, and completely removed from their caregiver responsibilities. You need to find ways to sustain yourself for the long haul.

I'm always aware of how much joy I get out of physical activity, of being able to take Will places easily, to hop on a subway in New York, go to a museum. When we plan something as a family, there's the whole logistical thing: going in back entrances, making special arrangements, things like that. I'm so aware and appreciative of how easy things are for me. If I were in bed and couldn't get up and couldn't go outside, I think it would just kill me. And that's what Chris goes through.

Chris is very conscious of remaining a vibrant, vital part of the family. He's a giving husband and a partner. And we place the same demands on one another that we've always placed on each other. Each of us has to live up to the other's expectations every day. It's how we live.

We have a terrific relationship. It took some doing. We didn't get married until five years after we met. Two of those years were a flurry of love and romance. The other years were knock-down, drag-out, working out all the junk and making sure we both had equal footing, real give-and-take. We knew it wouldn't always be pretty and perfect, and we talked about how we had to be there for each other. We hammered all that out so that by the time we got married, our eyes were wide open, and we were more in love than ever and really knew that we were choosing a partner for a lifetime—to go through the hard times with, to survive the tough stuff with.

I never would have asked for something like this to happen. And yet, the fact is, it did not stop our life. It changed the direction of our life.

I never would have asked for something like this to happen. And yet, the fact is, it did not stop our life. It changed the direction of our life. I'm surprised in retrospect, how much joy we still have in our life. I think if someone had presented this scenario to me and said my husband would be in a sudden, very debilitating accident, I would not have felt that I would have been able to cope with the situation at all, or that our life could have any happiness. And I think that's what a lot of people imagine. It actually turned out to be quite the contrary.

There are real gifts that come along with the hardships, and, if not for Chris's accident, I'm not sure we would have ever known these. We have a tremendous amount of joy in our family, a tremendous amount of laughter. We're a very close family. For example, one small thing: Chris isn't well today so he has to stay in bed. This means we'll have dinner in the bedroom. We'll sit in a circle around the bed because we want to have our meal together. We'll have a pleasant dinner hour together. It will make Chris feel good. It keeps us living and sharing as a family. And it sends a powerful message that no matter what your physical condition, you are a valued member of the family and we're going to carry on in our way together.

We're all so grateful for a beautiful day, so grateful for sunshine, for a day when Chris can be outside and not feel cold. I don't mean to sound like everyone isn't thankful for a beautiful day, but there is something about the fact that we've learned to truly appreciate the simple things, and I know I can experience joy and happiness even during difficult times. That's certainly one very powerful insight, and I don't think anyone could have told me that this was true. I've learned that you must live your life fully and well and truly appreciate what you've got.

There are real gifts that come along with the hardships, and, if not for Chris's accident, I'm not sure we would have ever known these.

This change in our lives has affected our son Will. He's become incredibly caring about other people. He's very physically affectionate, very concerned that other people's feelings and needs are taken care of, and he's wonderfully giving. He's also very accepting of people regardless of what they look like, what they can or cannot do; I think all of this is a result of living with a father who has a disability. I make a conscious effort not to present the world as a fearful and dangerous place. And yet the other side of that is that anything can happen. Accidents can happen to anyone.

Both Chris and I have learned something about parenting from our situation. So much of parenting is being there for the child. It's not so much being able to throw a ball with a child, for example, as sharing the child's experience, being there to support the child in throwing the ball. And then there's the big lesson. One of the greatest tools we can give our children is the capacity to deal with hardship and still have a happy life. We've been given this gift just by virtue of the fact that this accident happened. Life is going to be painful at times; we're all going to have our pain, loss, frustration, and hardship. The best things we can give our children are the tools to cope. You can adapt, you can find ways to be happy, and these are tremendously valuable lessons.

We have, whether we like it or not, become role models. And that's both a burden and a gift. If we perceive it more as a gift and less as a burden, it feels better. We've been given a caregiver's soap box. The system is not recognizing the reality of family caregivers—by "family caregivers" I mean a person responsible for the care of a spouse, parent, child, or other family member who is disabled or ill. That responsibility isn't officially recognized, not even on the census form. We need to start changing the system to provide some kind of financial aid for the job. The amount of money that family caregivers are saving the healthcare system by taking this responsibility on is enormous. What a wonderful thing it would be if we could, as a society, acknowledge these values—wanting to keep the care of family members in the family, wanting to take care of our own. I really feel gratified that, in speaking out, Chris and I are able to make a difference, and that's another gift we've received as a result of our situation.

One of the greatest tools we can give our children is the capacity to deal with hardship and still have a happy life.

11/29/04

DAVID CAWLEY

*When I visited David in his New York condominium, it
had only been three months since his partner John had died
of complications from AIDS. They had been together seven
years; David's first partner died over ten years earlier. For
fifteen years, David has worked in the music industry for
ASCAP, the American Society of Composers, Authors, and
Publishers. It's a field he enjoys because music is a big part
of his life. Because John's death was so recent, David was
barely back in his normal work routine. "It takes time to
heal," David told me. He had grown from his caregiving
experiences, but it had been "hard-earned wisdom." In a
choked voice and with sadness in his eyes, David said, "I
want to tell you my story, our story." And so he began.*

We were both HIV-positive when we met. In the
seven years I had known John, he was sick on and
off, but he'd bounced back from serious bouts
before. We both naively believed he'd come through the

recent setback he was experiencing. But this time he didn't get any stronger. Gradually over the last six months of his life, John lost a great deal of weight, couldn't eat solid foods, and couldn't swallow. When he came home from the hospital for the last time, he needed a suction machine, tube feedings, and the help of a home care worker. The last couple of months I slept on the sofa bed because John's hours were erratic and the machines were so noisy. John died three months ago. The cancer had metastasized; he developed pneumonia and went into cardiac arrest.

As sick as John was, I must admit that we never looked at the situation realistically. He had rebounded so many times in the past, even from a stroke three years ago, that we never anticipated he might not recover. I guess I expected that because so many medical advances had come about in recent years there would be something new to pull him through. It was terrible for me when I realized that neither medical help nor anything I could do would save him. I

We weren't acknowledging, even in the last days, that he might not recover. Maybe it's just human nature to hide in denial.

think because we both were avoiding reality we didn't take care of the practical things we should have. John's estate is now going to probate, our condo is going to have to be sold—all this on top of the loss and grief I deal with every day. This is a hard time for me. We weren't acknowledging, even in the last days, that he might not recover. Maybe it's just human nature to hide in denial. Anyhow, that's how we coped.

The last day that John was here at home, he asked me to lie down beside him. I'm crying now when I look back on that day. I think he realized he was close to dying and wouldn't be coming back home from his next trip to the hospital. These were our last moments of intimacy. Even at the end, the love between us was as strong as it had ever been. When they took John off life support, he kept breathing on his own for most of the week. Some of his family and friends kept a vigil night and day. At some point, I could see I needed some time off, and I went home and was alone for the first time in days. I sat there and realized that I couldn't go on holding my breath. I relaxed for the first time, and I felt that John could relax then and let go. I had been in suspended animation, on the edge, in a daze, in a twilight zone for days; and now, unexpectedly, I felt like myself for the first time.

I'm doing what I have to do now to make things easier for myself. I write in my journal about the pain I'm feeling when I'm in the depths of my grief and depression. It helps to get it out on the page. I'm in an online cancer caregivers' support group, and through it I've become friendly with a man whose wife of fifty years had cancer and another man who's the primary caregiver for his mother. My connection with these men, although I might never actually meet them, has been supportive.

I've grown both from my caregiving experiences and the grief and loss I've endured. It's been hard-earned wisdom. I trust there will be good things in my life ahead, so I hold on.

People have been reaching out to me here in the community, and that's a gratifying thing. I've had some dinner invitations, and the woman next door got two of her friends to come over one day to clean the apartment. That was during a time when I just couldn't get it together. The people I work with raised money in the office to help pay some of the funeral expenses, and others in the neighborhood inquire how I'm doing. My parents live in Florida, so I haven't seen them since John's death, but they've been very supportive. They call often.

When people I know ask what they can do for me, I tell them to call me and suggest something specific. I'd like it a lot if they'd come and visit, or we could go to dinner. It's hard for me to initiate a call to someone and ask them to do something for me. During the first couple of weeks there were a lot of messages on the phone machine and cards in the mail, but then that dropped off. But I continue to reach out to others— it's a survival technique that has rewards.

When you have a committed, loving relationship and expect to spend the remainder of your life with that person and death ends that, the loss is heavy and the grief is deep. Now that I'm alone, like so many others in similar situations, I have to learn how to nurture myself. I need to give myself the credit, love, and support that I've been giving to others. It's my nature to give, and I've been privileged to do that for two partners. In a sense, I gave each of my partners the best years of their lives. I've grown both from my caregiving experiences and the grief and loss I've endured. It's been hard-earned wisdom. I trust there will be good things in my life ahead, so I hold on. I hope I will love again. I have a lot of love to share.

ELBERT COLE

Serving as the caregiver to a loved one with Alzheimer's or any condition of mental deterioration can be a heart-wrenching, stressful, and confusing experience. To maintain a relationship of dignity and respect in the face of the personality and behavioral changes that often come with such illness is an enormous challenge. Elbert Cole is a Methodist minister but no longer the head of a congregation. When Elbert Cole's wife, Virginia, was diagnosed with Alzheimer's, he and their adult children devised a personal plan of caregiving that ultimately offered great rewards. They discussed her present condition, as well as the projected decline, as a family, divided up responsibilities, and made plans to live as normally as possible. Virginia lived for seventeen years with Alzheimer's. Elbert Cole talked with me about her life and her death.

B efore Virginia was diagnosed, there were symptoms that things were not right. Early on we met as a family—my two adult children and my wife Virginia as well. At this point, the deterioration was just beginning. We knew that if we really wanted to be helpful we needed to pursue not the dream of cure but the path of caregiving.

To stay informed, our son, who is a scientist, followed the latest research on Alzheimer's. If there were to be a cure, if there were to be some hope or relief, we wanted to know of it. We dedicated ourselves to finding ways of keeping Virginia looking well dressed and fashionable. My daughter took that on. Having given it some prior thought, I said to Virginia, "Why don't we have a contract? Suppose you take life on and see how much enjoyment you get from it, and then you let me manage life and see if I can handle that. Then let's judge each other and see who's doing the best job." We negotiated a new kind of partnership, and I decided she would go everywhere with me. I made no apologies and asked no permission. I pulled a chair up alongside of board tables and everywhere else, and she just sat there and enjoyed the whole proceeding. Her task was to enjoy.

We knew that if we really wanted to be helpful we needed to pursue not the dream of cure but the path of caregiving.

Instead of withdrawing from life and feeling that I should be ashamed, I felt proud of Virginia. I assumed that if people couldn't accept her condition then they had the problem, not her. I coached the children so they wouldn't worry if their mother was quiet when they called. It only meant that she was listening carefully to every word they were sharing with her. I advised them to keep on talking normally. Virginia would just sit and smile. She knew at the other end of the phone was somebody that loved her.

All people need to know they're loved, to feel good about themselves, be respected, feel secure, be included and not alienated or marginalized, celebrate the joy of life, and be needed. Having Alzheimer's doesn't change the need for such things. When you're dealing with someone who seems to be on a whole different level, a simple childlike level, it can become too easy to subordinate that person to an inferior position. If you don't respect the other person as a person, a being who still has something to contribute, then you can too easily begin treating them as a "thing," an object that must be dressed and fed rather than a person with whom you can share life.

Of course, it isn't always easy to do this. But by prematurely making other people's decisions, we may shut them off from the very sustenance of their own lives, dominate them. It's a balance to allow a continuation of freedom and yet take on the responsibility of being a caregiver. Caregiving is being alert to making life as good as possible for the other person.

Caregiving is being alert to making life as good as possible for the other person.

Virginia was different from many other people who have Alzheimer's. She was quiet, never demanding, always gracious and appreciative of what was done for her. It's amazing that she retained that capacity when you read the literature and hear of other situations. For me, for us as a family, she never was a burden. I tried to keep Virginia connected to the world and stimulated. She had a deep interest in art so we often went to museums. We walked through shopping centers to look at things. And she loved to talk with children. There were times, of course, when she'd do inappropriate things, like pat a man's backside or reach for a woman's purse or go over to strange children and pat their heads. But I never felt ashamed of Virginia; I never felt apologetic. I did occasionally have a wistful thought about how nice it would be if she (and we) had better years ahead, but on the other hand, we made the most of what we had.

We shared a lot. I loved traveling with her, spending time with her, going to meetings and speeches. And we laughed together. Humor is so important in life. It's healing. It's relaxing. It lightens things up, and it keeps you out of self-pity. When you're dealing with dementia, you're dealing with a world of fantasy and imagination, and there's richness and beauty in such places. I don't think it should be thought of as "bad." Sure, somebody needs to be around who knows where the real world is. Life can still be good for the person living partly in another reality.

Caregiving must never become an unmanageable burden. If it does, it's wrong, and the price on you will be too great. A person who has the responsibility to coordinate the care of a loved one has to know what they can handle and what they can't. There need be no guilt involved. You do what you need to do. For some, the burdens, frustrations, and adjustments are things they simply can't handle or don't choose to handle. In my situation, our family shared the challenges and reaped the rewards. Our whole family felt that Virginia continued to teach us so much all the way to the end. We discovered that there are all kinds of rewards that come, some quietly and unexpectedly. Virginia taught us how to slow down a little bit. She taught us a kind of a peace and a quiet courage. We all learned lessons from her. When you live with someone acting out their life with increasing limitations, you can't help but begin to rethink your own life and what's really important.

Caregiving must never become an unmanageable burden. If it does, it's wrong, and the price on you will be too great.

Once, when Virginia was quite weary, I decided I wouldn't take her along for my speech that evening. When I came back, she was lying on top of the bed with the light on, asleep. I leaned over, and she awoke with a childlike beaming smile on her face, knowing that her friend had come home. The next morning, as I was giving her a shower, she began to hyperventilate, and I knew that her life was terminating. Her strength and demeanor was such that she was obviously under some strain.

So I put her back on the bed and sat on the edge of the bed for two hours just watching her, talking to her about our history and our children and everything that we had accomplished in our lives together. And I told her how courageous I thought she had been, and what a wonderful wife and mother she had been. And she just lay there and watched me and smiled, and listened and listened and listened. And then finally she had no strength left, and the life just left her body.

I took her in my arms and started to recite the Twenty-third Psalm. I must admit, because of my emotion and tears, I skipped about every other line. I was grateful that we had had this time of privacy and that she had died in peace.

With all the stories of the difficulties of mental illness, it's easy to lose sight of the tenderness that people share with loved ones. For me, being able to celebrate the tenderness, talk about it, affirm it, and say *that's* what I remember became a real gift. And I think it was a gift for Virginia as well. We'd had fifty-four years of marriage. Her illness extended over seventeen of those years. I've not lingered much on what could have been. I know how wonderful it was that we continued to journey together, and maybe that was my greatest gift of all.

ELIZABETH MOODY

Although Elizabeth and Harry both had careers and were raising two young children, they took on the unique challenge of becoming caregivers, not for a family member but for an elderly friend, Mr. Morris. While many people take on the responsibility of care for a relative, it's uncommon for a busy couple with young children to assume the full-time care of a friend. Mr. Morris was in his nineties, had outlived two wives, had no children, and was living alone in an apartment not far from Elizabeth and Harry. For many years, Mr. Morris had been close friends with the couple and had become like a grandfather to their children. He began having meals with the family quite frequently, and over the course of a year, discussed the possibility of moving into an apartment adjoining their home, which he would pay to construct. The addition was planned and built, and Mr. Morris moved into his new quarters and became part of the family. Elizabeth tells of this unique experience of caregiving.

My husband and I wanted to give something back for all we had been given in our lives. We talked it over and decided to ask Mr. Morris if he would like to come and live with us. We really wanted him to be here, and we were ready to assume the responsibility of what care he needed. At that time, our long-time family friend was about ninety-one. He'd outlived everybody that he knew; he had never had any children. When his late wife had a stroke, he was her caregiver for three years. Now he needed someone to make life comfortable for him.

We built the addition onto our house; it was to be his own little apartment where he had his own kitchen. Mr. Morris stayed with us for six years. And during the first few years he really was quite independent. He actually did a little driving, and he usually would fix his own breakfast and lunch. He would join the family for dinner. It was a wonderful opportunity for him to spend time with young children, which he never really had done much of in his life. It was a great thing for the children, who loved him dearly. It was just fine with them that Mr. Morris had all the time in the world, not like their parents who were always in a hurry to get somewhere or get something done.

We talk of how important it is to live in the moment. Sometimes we say this blithely, not really understanding what it means; but when you're forced by your circumstances to slow down your life to the pace of someone who really does live in the moment, it changes your life.

Gradually, Mr. Morris became somewhat frail, and during the last year that he was with us he was actually bedridden or in a wheelchair. We became full-time caregivers as he then required a great deal of care. Fortunately, we have a large group of friends, and Mr. Morris actually knew many of them. An old friend of his was a nurse and lived only a few blocks away. Another was a physician who made house calls to Mr. Morris. There were some men we know who would take turns bathing him. There were maybe two or three who would come at different times and do that chore. So we really didn't do this all by ourselves. We had the very meaningful support of a large group of friends who were also caring people. This provided respite for us, so to speak. We had all the bases covered.

My time with Mr. Morris taught me a great deal. We talk of how important it is to live in the moment. Sometimes we say this blithely, not really understanding what it means; but when you're forced by your circumstances to slow down your life to the pace of someone who really does live in the moment, it changes your life. I would wake Mr. Morris up about 9:30 in the morning. And it would take me until about 11:30 to get him his breakfast, dress him, comb his hair, help him with his teeth, and situate him in his wheelchair so that he could sit comfortably. That would take about two hours. But in those two hours, we would live each moment. I found it a humbling experience to know that I had that to learn.

I knew this thing we were going through together could be a horrible thing, a drudgery, or together we could make it a deeply meaningful experience.

There were times when I gave into impatience and irritation, and I'm sure the tone in my voice wasn't gracious or kind. I'd hear myself saying something that was irritable and impatient, and that would snap me back into the reality of the situation. I knew this thing we were going through together could be a horrible thing, a drudgery, or together we could make it a deeply meaningful experience. Remembering that made it easy for me to make the experience something special and kind. And Mr. Morris, too, would bring kindness and consideration into the morning. I'd be cranking up his bed, which was hard physically, and he'd often say something like, "Oh, that's such hard work for you, I hope you don't hurt your back. Please be careful." In such caring exchanges we made our day mean more than a morning of chores. The reality was that Mr. Morris and I were partners, we were in this caregiving thing together, and we learned from each other.

I discovered that there are many ways you can approach each moment. We all do so much in our lives that ultimately hasn't much meaning. I think if you can focus on the present, and truly know the value of doing something for someone that's good, something this person really needs right now, and you can do that good thing, everybody wins. I'm speaking about the essential quality of goodness, not excellence. I'm finding it difficult to explain this. I just know that service to others expands one's life and adds beauty. There's a man who lives on my street, a retired scientist, and every day I see him out walking and pushing the wheelchair of one of our neighbors. I see them walking and talking and enjoying one another. I feel I have a bond with this man. He understands.

Service to others expands one's life and adds beauty.

And as I look back on it now, those were the best years of my life. It was a blessing for us to care for Mr. Morris. It was an absolute gift. You know, there aren't that many opportunities that people have in their life to give back, and this was ours. Mr. Morris would not have had the comfort and dignity he deserved if he hadn't come to stay with us, but we were the winners in this situation. It's easy to be helpful when the need is clear. The way I try to live my life, I see service as a gift. I had the opportunity to step in and help and that was a gift.

EVIE ROSEN-BUDD

Bill has multiple sclerosis. At the time of our conversation, Bill's wife, Evie, was sixty-eight and Bill was seventy-nine. For many couples, retirement is a time to travel and explore new things. Yet, for couples like Evie and Bill, illness and limitations prevent pursuing such adventures. Recently, Evie and Bill moved from their Northern California retirement community to Colorado to live closer to their adult children. The decision was difficult, yet everyone realized that Evie and Bill needed their family's help and support. I've known Evie and Bill for many years, so I was comfortable taking my tape recorder along on a visit and asking Evie to talk about her caregiving experience. Here's what she told me.

Where should I begin? My husband Bill has multiple sclerosis. When I married him, I knew he had multiple sclerosis, but I had no idea what I was getting into. It was the second marriage for both of us. People warned us about the possibilities of total disability, but it was too late—we were madly in love. Bill was diagnosed with MS in 1980. We were married in 1984. He was still walking then with a bit of an uneven gait; he soon began using a cane, then a walker, a scooter, and, ten years ago, a wheelchair. When Bill first went into a wheelchair, he could operate it himself. Over the years he's lost the use of his hands, so he has to be fed, bathed, and transferred in and out of bed. We have an automobile that has a conversion for the wheelchair, so we're able to get around. I'm strong enough to load and unload Bill and the wheelchair wherever we go. It's our lifeline, our access to the world. We decided a long time ago that we were going to use some of our savings to make our lives easier. The van was expensive, and I remember thinking we should be saving money for that "rainy day," and Bill said, "Maybe this is it."

My life is totally organized around the care that Bill needs. As his disease changes and alters his needs, my caregiving responsibilities change as well.

I've been a caregiver in some measure all of these years. My life is totally organized around the care that Bill needs. As his disease changes and alters his needs, my caregiving responsibilities change as well. Bill is considered a quadriplegic. I'm responsible for all of his daily living activities. I give Bill a shower, transferring him with a patient lift to a shower chair and back in bed to dress him. I brush his teeth, change his catheter, make his meals, feed him, read to him, order books on tape for him to listen to, take him to movies, try to visit friends if their homes are accessible, and on and on. Thankfully, he has a bright mind and no cognitive impairment.

We have an aide who comes in three mornings a week, gives him a shower and a shave, and does some physical therapy with him; the other four days a week, I get him out of bed, dress him, and take care of him. Just to give you an idea of some of our expenses: the aide is thirty dollars an hour. On the mornings the aide is here, I'm able to leave for a couple of hours and take the dog for a run. Then I come back and get ready for the day. I'm here for all of our meals. A lot of days we eat only two meals; we don't have a set routine. The thing that has changed most, and I don't remember quite when this happened, is that I can't leave Bill alone and I'm no longer able to get away for short periods of time on my own. The hardest part for me as a caregiver is not having the ease of spontaneously getting away. The challenge is finding the right person to stay here when I leave, and the other concern is the cost.

The truth is that I really don't enjoy being away from Bill. I much prefer to take him with me, but that's not always possible because not every place I want to go is accessible to him; but I much, much prefer to have him with me. We do have an extraordinary relationship; it's very open, we're able to resolve issues. Yes, Bill is dependent, but we need to make decisions together to have our relationship work.

The hardest part for me as a caregiver is not having the ease of spontaneously getting away.

People sometimes ask, who takes care of me? This caregiver takes care of the caregiver! That's very, very important. It's right up there with taking care of Bill. I take good care of myself and I keep busy. I do some hiking, exercising, yoga, grocery shopping—anything that helps me to get some time on my own and keep a positive attitude so I can carry on my caregiving responsibilities. And I get a lot of support from Bill. He encourages me to take care of myself, to work out, to take time to do for myself what I need to do. I work some, too, out of my home office. I'm the resource editor for the National Family Caregivers Association. I review books, tapes, products, and services, and write the resource page for our newsletter. It helps me to keep informed as well as help others. Occasionally, I'm asked to speak or do a workshop, and sometimes Bill and I do a presentation together for local groups.

One positive aspect of my caregiving is that I feel useful, important. It's a very good feeling to have an opportunity, right here in my own house to make a difference, and that's rewarding. There are times, of course, when others need to help me—when there's a medical problem or something complex that I can't understand. I enjoy trying to figure some things out for myself, though. Sometimes, when something in our house isn't working properly or a piece of Bill's equipment is broken, Bill says, "Call somebody," and I'll say, "No wait. Let me see if I can figure it out first." I like to figure out how to fix something, how to solve a problem, how to make whatever Bill needs work better for him. That helps me feel needed and useful and competent.

I do have times when I get frustrated and irritated. But

> *One positive aspect of my caregiving is that I feel useful, important. It's a very good feeling to have an opportunity right here in my own house to make a difference.*

that doesn't have to do with Bill. It's when equipment breaks down, or repair people don't show up, or we've hired somebody and they can't do what they said they could—that kind of thing. My frustrating, irritating, dark times are usually connected with equipment not working, how much money it takes for the care Bill needs, or how to find and keep competent help. Then there's the continuing difficulty of dealing with the healthcare system. When I get sick (although that doesn't happen very often) or when Bill gets sick, sometimes I just lose it. I get scared that I can't handle it, and sometimes I scream and yell and say nasty, mean things. I remember once I screamed, "Maybe you should be in a nursing home," which, of course, I didn't really mean. It doesn't happen often, but when I act out like this Bill just gets very quiet, closes his eyes, and lets me rant and rave. And then I feel totally drained, and the episode is over and I'm okay again.

Last October, Bill was rushed to the hospital with what we thought was a stroke but turned out to be a raging bladder infection that had to be watched carefully. When people with MS get any kind of an infection, their whole system shuts down. The scene in the emergency room was so frightening and frustrating for me. I was trying to be calm, but it was difficult for me not knowing if Bill was going to be okay. They wanted to catheterize him and give him a broad spectrum antibiotic and other treatments, but before I'd agree to anything I wanted an explanation and more information. The medical personnel wanted me to leave the room, but I wouldn't go. I was exhausted and furious.

People ask, how do I do it? We do it one day at a time.

I finally got through to them, but if I hadn't been persistent, aggressive, and informed it wouldn't have happened. They simply do not understand the role of the family caregiver. Our coverage entitled Bill to home healthcare after being released from the hospital. They sent over nursing help that was inept and totally inexperienced with someone in Bill's condition. I could hardly stand it. I could yell and scream all I wanted—but that was who was available and that's who they sent. It's situations such as this that get me down. The healthcare system is a source of great frustration to us much of the time.

People ask, how do I do it? I don't think of it like that. We do it one day at a time. What's changed over the years is that we've had increasing limitations so we've had to supplement, or sublimate, or—I don't know what the correct word would be—substitute, maybe. We manage to find ways to entertain ourselves and do some of the things we enjoy, while letting go of other things. I look at my life as a caregiver in a positive way. Most of the time it is, about eighty/twenty. I think Bill, who's the care recipient, feels the same way. About 80 percent of the time he sees his life in a positive way, and then 20 percent of the time there are other feelings. That would be a good enough attitude for any of us in life.

I find caregiving for Bill challenging but extraordinarily gratifying. I know I'm making a difference in his life, and that's where my gratification comes from. I feel so much joy while watching him get pleasure out of what we're doing together. My caregiving isn't a frustrating task for me because it gives me a great deal back. I think it's because of the person I'm giving the care to.

Bill is an extraordinary guy. He's always willing to learn. He's a lot of fun. He has an open, inquisitive mind, and that gives me a lot. He's an inspiration for me. There's great love and affection here. I truly feel like we're doing this together. I don't feel alone. Bill gives me tremendous affirmation as a woman, a wife, a mother, and a grandmother; he's very affirming of everything I do. He exudes love for me, constantly telling me how wonderful I am. One night we went out to a concert, and during intermission a man we didn't know came over and said to me, "I've been watching you and your husband. It touches my heart to see so much love. Your affection for each other truly shows." That he would come over to us and say such things really amazed me. If people have some purpose in this world, maybe this is ours: to show people what true love looks like.

I'm learning that I can be patient. There are also deeper rewards, spiritual rewards, that have come for me as a caregiver. Millions of people in our world need help. I have only one person to help but, in a way, it's like helping the whole

> *Millions of people in our world need help. I have only one person to help but, in a way, it's like helping the whole world.*

world. It feels good inside to help someone else, whether that's someone who is disabled like Bill, or somebody on the street who is homeless, or even by sending money to cancer research. I'm fortunate enough to be reminded of it every minute of every day.

Sometimes I say to myself, "What would I be doing with my life if I wasn't doing this?" I don't feel deprived. People are always telling me they admire me. People come up to me that I don't even know. Actually, what I do isn't that hard. It's time consuming, sure, but this is my life, after all. I don't want people to misunderstand and think that this is easy. It's not easy; but it is doable.

The biggest reward of caregiving for me is finding out what's really important in life and focusing on that. I'm not preoccupied by or encumbered with possessions. It's more important for us just to share our lives together than to have material things. As a result of being a caregiver, I feel competent and confident. When I'm out with other people and they're dressed nicer than I am or they look more put together, I'm okay with that. I know who I am, and I found this out through caregiving. I know where my priorities are, what my values are. I feel so good that I don't need those other things. That's my reward.

The biggest reward of caregiving for me is finding out what's really important in life and focusing on that.

There's an intimacy about caregiving that I enjoy. Our giving and taking has mutuality; we're partners in caregiving. I don't think this is always the way it is between caregivers and the people being cared for.

From time to time, I'll see couples walking arm in arm and wonder what that would feel like. But then I also see people dealing with heart disease, cancer, hearing loss, sight loss, and any number of ailments and ills, and I wonder what that would be like. Would I be able to deal with that?

Recently, I read a sentence that really spoke to me: "I live the life that is before me." That's it. That's what I do.

What I've gained through caregiving is a deep and profound understanding of compassion—compassion, not just for the person I care for, but for everyone who needs caregiving, for everyone who gives care. It's my deepest learning, my greatest gift.

FAITH HEINEMANN

One day, my phone rang and a friend said, "I heard that you were interviewing family caregivers. Here's my friend Faith's phone number. Call her." So I did and went to see Faith at her charming Malibu beach house. What might have seemed on the surface like an ordinary afternoon of tea and conversation was, for me, nothing ordinary at all. I was inspired by what Faith had to say. I don't recall at what point in our conversation she repeated the words of Eleanor Roosevelt, but the quote captures the essence of Faith's caregiving story: "You gain strength, courage, and confidence by every experience in which you really stop to look fear in the face.... You must do the thing you think you cannot do."

We had always affectionately called my husband "Albert, the absent-minded professor," so I didn't think too much about his growing lack of memory. Because he had always been a complete rebel, I rationalized that he just didn't care what others thought and didn't bother to remember what they said. Albert was a marvelous architect. He made the most beautiful designs. I was working then; my office was downtown in the Federal Building. I'd go to work and leave him at home to work on his drawings and plans.

Then strange things began happening. He flooded the kitchen with the garden hose. He began to wander and get lost. Albert was aware something wasn't right, and he was concerned about it. He became leery of strangers and was easily upset, even violent. The wandering became more frequent. Then he had a car accident. One day, a friend was visiting and quietly suggested to me, "Maybe you should take Albert for some neurological tests." The result was a diagnosis of Alzheimer's. I was devastated.

At first, I had this feeling of, "Oh, my God, what have I taken on? Can I do this?" Yet, in my heart I knew that for me it was the right thing to do.

I tried to both work and manage Albert, but it wasn't very long before I discovered that it was more than I could handle. To make a long story short, I quit my job to stay home and care for him. My son became terribly concerned that I was exhausting myself and insisted I put Albert in a nursing home. Albert was in the home for about three months. It broke my heart to see him tied into a chair and on heavy tranquilizers; he was like a zombie. I finally decided I would do everything I had to do to care for him at home. The day I picked him up and we pulled in front of the house, the first thing he said was, "I'm home, I'm home."

It all seemed overwhelming. At first, I had this feeling of, "Oh, my God, what have I taken on? Can I do this?" Yet, in my heart I knew that for me it was the right thing to do. I tapered off his medications one at a time, and after a while I completely stopped all the drugs. He gradually calmed

down. My husband was a big, tall, strong man, so he needed help from someone who was also big and strong.
Fortunately I could afford to employ some male nursing
assistants from a local agency to come in for a few hours
each day, so I had some respite. Albert had lost the ability to
walk and was falling all the time. He couldn't feed himself
very well, and very soon he couldn't even talk. I moved him
into a room on the main level of the house and made it into
a warm, welcoming area. I had posters on the wall and fresh
flowers in the room, and there was a little deck outside
where Albert could sit in the sun and have his meals.

The man I knew and loved and who had been a very important part of my life was gradually drifting away. I needed to focus on all those joyous and satisfying years we had shared. I'll never really lose him if I can hold on to what we had together.

I began to realize that I had
to have some time away, time to
be refreshed, so I could come
back and deal with it all. I
began to go out to lunch, take a
swim in the community pool,
go shopping, or just take the
dog for a walk. One of the
things I learned very quickly
was that to be a good and loving caregiver, you have to take
care of yourself.

At some point, rather early on, I began keeping a diary.
At the beginning, what was primarily on my mind was loss.
The man I knew and loved and who had been a very important part of my life was gradually drifting away. The essence
of this person I knew so well was eroding; he was quickly dis-
appearing, and I needed to write about the loss. I also felt a
need to write about the many wonderful things we had done
together. I needed to focus on all those joyous and satisfying
years we had shared. I'll never really lose him if I can hold on
to what we had together. I'll always have these beautiful
memories. I needed to write about my memories and feeling.

My diary eventually became a book called *A Different Reality: An Alzheimer's Love Story.*

All forms of dementia are horrible, tragic. They rob a person of their personality, the whole essence of a person's being changes, and the one you love disappears before your eyes. My comfort has come from my faith. It isn't the answer for everyone, but the Catholic Church gave me what I needed. I love the ritual and the ceremony. It connects me to a higher power, and I personally need that. My faith gave me some peace and helped me through the whole experience.

Yet, it was a day-to-day struggle. Through it all I began to look at love in a different way, in an entirely deeper sense. So often when we think of love the image is of romance and joy. I began to wonder why we don't see beauty in some of those things about life that we usually perceive as ugly. For example, my husband's body was gradually coming apart—a beautiful, strong body was becoming old and feeble. Was this really something ugly? As I watched Albert fail and deteriorate, something touched my heart so deeply that I loved him more than ever. I learned that the beauty of love is often in something that other people might call the ugly side of life, the side we don't want to see. It was a dramatic transition for me to see that I loved Albert more completely, more honestly, more deeply than I ever thought possible. This change of perspective helped me to get through the whole thing. I was so grateful that I could be there with him the whole time.

I learned that the beauty of love is often in something that other people might call the ugly side of life, the side we don't want to see. It was a dramatic transition for me to see that I loved Albert more completely, more honestly, more deeply than I ever thought possible.

It was particularly hard as the end came near. A friend of mine suggested that I should contact our local hospice.

Having their help was the most wonderful experience I have ever had. I can't say enough good things about hospice. Everyone was marvelous and wonderfully supportive; they offered the understanding and sympathy that we needed. The family was all here, friends came, and this small but close group surrounded Albert with love. I sat by him and held his hand, and he squeezed mine, opened his eyes, and said, "I love you." It was a peaceful death.

It's been two years since my husband died. I now lead support groups for caregivers. In fact, I started doing this while I was caring for Albert. Here is how it came about. For years I worked as an economist, as Chief of the Los Angeles office with the Bureau of Labor Statistics. I was allowed to work a four-day week, and I went back to school to study to become a therapist. The Bureau of Labor Statistics actually paid for a lot of the training because they knew it was useful for employees who were having emotional upheavals, alcohol problems, and other psychological stresses.

I can't say enough good things about hospice. Everyone was marvelous and wonderfully supportive; they offered the understanding and sympathy that we needed.

One day, I was walking my dog and encountered another woman with her dog. She was crying and was absolutely distraught. I discovered in talking with her that her husband had Alzheimer's. She didn't know what to do, who to talk with, where to get help. I contacted the priest at my church and suggested leading a support group for people who were caring for family members. The group consisted entirely of women who were caring for their husbands. It was wonderfully cohesive and supportive. We learned a lot from one another. We helped each other enormously. Anyone could feel comfortable expressing anything they felt. It was a safe place. I think the biggest thing we discovered was that we could really count on one another. After Albert died, I started another group as well. I had been through the whole process during the seven years of Albert's illness, and now I felt I could help others through the various emotional stages of their caregiving challenges, their loss and grief, and after a time, their healing.

One of the most significant things I've learned from all of this is that I'm strong. I never would have believed that before. I wasn't confident that I was competent, resilient, and strong. Having gone through all this, having chosen the path of a caregiver, I'm much more secure and confident. I feel I can handle new challenges and find my place in the world.

FRAN KIRKHAM

"I'm fifty-six now," Fran told me as we began our conversation. "It's about time I let go of the pain and the sadness and move on." She was talking about an old emotional wound, one that wasn't healed before her father died. I think it's important to share her story because it reminds us that not being able to repair a damaged relationship with a dying parent can profoundly affect a surviving child's life. Fran talked about her experience in the hope that her story will help others.

It was ten years ago that my dad died. I came into my caregiving role unexpectedly. I was living in Japan and teaching English as a second language. I had no idea that my dad was sick. One day, out of the blue, I got a call from my aunt telling me that my dad had had a lung biopsy and been diagnosed with advanced lung cancer. She told me to come home quickly, so my husband and I packed up and left Japan. My dad lived only a couple of weeks after our arrival.

Dad insisted on being at home those last few weeks. He was eighty years old, in a great deal of pain, and seemed ready to get out of this world as quickly as possible. To him, being in a hospital and getting any kind of treatment only prolonged the inevitable. He didn't want strangers in his house. He was fearful that anyone coming in to help might prolong his life. And he was suspicious of everything, even pain medication. I didn't know how to care for a dying person, and I didn't know anyone in the community to ask for help. I tried to convince Dad to let hospice come to the house and help, but he absolutely refused. The most difficult thing for me was facing this all alone.

I wasn't emotionally ready to tackle the caregiver role, and not at all prepared psychologically for dealing with my father. There were many unresolved issues between us. The unsatisfying quality of those few weeks we spent together as he was dying still hangs over me. It's sad that both my dad's and my experience of those last days of his life couldn't have been a time of reconciliation and healing.

I didn't know how to care for a dying person, and I didn't know anyone in the community to ask for help. The most difficult thing for me was facing this all alone.

My father and I had spent our lives butting heads. As a child and a teenager, I didn't understand him and he didn't understand me. Layers of anger and hurt had built up between us. I had been raised in a home where we didn't talk about things, certainly never about feelings and emotions. My father's life was colored by many losses, and I now understand how this shaped who he was. His mother committed suicide when he was fifteen, and he was sent away to military school. His father died of a heart attack soon after I was born. My mother died a few years later. Dad remarried very quickly after my mother's death, and his second wife died within a year. My brother died of cancer at age eighteen, and at age twenty, I ran off and married someone he didn't approve of. I remember thinking that maybe if I had a child, if I made my dad a grandfather, some of the hurt would heal. So I got pregnant and found in the middle of my term that I had a very rare form of cancer that you only get when you're pregnant: choriocarcinoma. The placenta reproduces cells incorrectly and kills the fetus. For me, it was a life-threatening illness. My recovery was long and slow.

That my dad wanted me to come and be with him in his last days—and that I didn't hesitate to come—might indicate we both wanted some healing of our relationship. It was sad that we didn't know how to make that happen. My dad didn't want me to see him as a sick and dying old man, and I had never been around death and didn't know how to deal with it. He was never the kind of person to talk about emotions, so he didn't share his thoughts and feelings with me. I was unable at the time to deal with the residual anger that had piled up all those years, so I too was unable to reach out. Neither of us could talk to each other in a meaningful way.

That my dad wanted me to come and be with him in his last days—and that I didn't hesitate to come—might indicate we both wanted some healing of our relationship. It was sad that we didn't know how to make that happen.

My dad died without our saying good-bye to each other, without our saying that, in spite of it all, we loved each other. Sadly, there was this incredible silence that hung between us. I don't remember even touching him. The healing that might have been possible never happened. To have my dad die without any reconciliation between us has been a heavy emotional road for me to travel these ten years since his death.

In recent years, some healing has come for me through a new understanding of who he was and why he reacted to me as he did throughout his life. As I look at his life, so full of loss, I have some understanding of his inability to connect with people. I can remember him now with a tenderness and loving feeling that I could never experience when he was alive.

After my father's death, I felt strongly that I had to find a different path of work. Teaching English and living in a foreign country no longer felt right for me. I craved a new direction that included work that touched my heart, my feelings. I needed work that would help me heal and allow me to help others. One day, a friend came to talk to me about an idea for a project that she wanted to create: a series of workshops around the death of a mother. It was as if an inner voice said, "This is what you've been looking for."

Together we created a series of workshops and groups called HEALING HEARTS. Our work is different from other grief support groups in that we only assist people who are having difficulties dealing with the death of a parent. Many of the people we work with are older, and it may have been many years since their loss. It's not unusual for both men and women to be working out feelings related to the loss of a parent many years after it has happened. Suddenly the sadness, the guilt, and the grief resurface, as mine did. I feel that in many ways what I'm doing with my life now is exactly what I should be doing. My personal history of loss provides me with a way to help others with issues surrounding the loss of a parent.

Walking with other people through their journeys makes me realize that it's never too late and that we should not close the door to any opportunity for change and growth.

What have I learned from all this? Well, I've learned that you can heal a relationship with a parent even after his or her death. I've learned that if someone experiences continual loss, it affects their life and the lives of those around them profoundly. I'm gratified that I can help other people face things similar to what I've faced and that I can heal myself by helping them. This is what my life purpose is. Walking with other people through their journeys makes me realize that it's never too late and that we should not close the door to any opportunity for change and growth. The opportunity can come from an unexpected place.

HEALING HEARTS is an enterprise that will never make us rich. But it doesn't matter, really. It's not the reason I'm doing this. If it ever becomes something that puts making money first, then I'll know it's time for me to get out. It's work that for me is life affirming, heart centered, and spiritually fulfilling.

FRANCIS BATTISTI

Francis Battisti is married and has three grown sons. He lives in upstate New York and is a professor of psychology, education, and human services in New York's state university system. In addition to maintaining a counseling practice, he presents seminars and workshops around the country on various aspects of midlife transition.

That's the kind of information you'll find in his resumé. But Francis would rather talk about his dad and his experience as a caregiver. Being a caregiver during the last years of his father's life brought about many personal realizations for Francis. "My relationship with my dad those years of his illness fed my own midlife growing experience," he told me. Here's his story.

My father lived in the family home that my grandfather had built, which he was very attached to. I helped him maintain his independence and live there as long as I could. My dad was always self-sufficient, but when he became ill, he needed help, and I took on the role of caregiver.

I wanted everything in my father's care to be perfect. I was determined to be the perfect caregiver. Eventually, I saw that there were many things connected with his illness that I had no control over, but at that time, I thought that if I handled it all perfectly I could make him well. I was going to do everything right and keep him alive another ten or more years. I was so busy making things right that I didn't acknowledge reality. The truth was that he knew he was going to die.

I don't know how or when it happened, but I came to accept that my dad wasn't going to get well, that I couldn't fix him. Somehow, I had touched on the wisdom to know that all my efforts might make him comfortable but I couldn't make him well.

For months I was involved in "doing." I had to constantly be doing something for my dad. I would get done working at the college, see my private clients, get to my dad's house at 7:00 at night, make his dinner, change his bed, do the laundry, give him his medication, clean the house, get his meals ready for the next day and leave a little after 9:00. I'd do that every night.

One day, I realized that I was trying to fix everything. I don't know how or when it happened, but I came to accept that my dad wasn't going to get well, that I couldn't fix him. Somehow, I had touched on the wisdom to know that all my efforts might make him comfortable but I couldn't make him well. Then I was ready to learn another lesson.

Every once in a while my dad would say, "Hey, Francis, why don't you sit down with me and talk?" But I'd always say, "No time for that, Dad. Sorry." I had gotten caught up in doing stuff around the house, in the routine care of my dad. Then one day I was driving home and it suddenly hit me. My dad was asking me to stop doing the "stuff" and to sit down with him, talk with him, share with him my day, and simply let him express his thoughts. He was asking me to listen to him. And when this hit me a voice in my head said, "Hey, I'm so busy 'doing' that I've got no time for 'being.'" I suddenly became aware that this was an opportunity that would never come again. Anyone could do the household stuff, but no one could be with my dad like I could, and there was no person in the world who could be with me like he could.

So things changed. I started to get other people to do the chores so that when I came over to the house I could just be with him. We would go out to lunch and just spend time together talking. There were a lot of things I wanted to know about him and the family, and to understand before he died. As we talked more and more, I felt I was touching my roots in a way I never had before. I felt like I was a little kid again.

Anyone could do the household stuff, but no one could be with my dad like I could, and there was no person in the world who could be with me like he could.

These were our best times together. We talked about his early childhood, and I began to understand my father in a different way. My father's father, my grandfather, left Italy when my father was five, and he worked in the United States for about ten years. When my father was ten, his father brought him to the United States. After only one year, his father went back to Italy, saying he'd return with the rest of the family. But he didn't, and my dad never saw him again. I began to get a deeper understanding of who my father was, how his childhood and early years had shaped him.

My dad was thinking deeply about the meaning of his life, his values, the way he had conducted his business, and how proud he was of what he had accomplished. We talked about family, and I told him how much he had given me and how much our getting close in these last months had meant to me. We talked about his mother, whom he hadn't seen since he was a child. He said he was dreaming about her a lot, maybe because he knew he was dying and would be seeing her soon. That's when I started to cry, and he teared up, too. Italian men aren't supposed to cry, but we were both deeply touched. We had entered another level of our relationship, a kind of intimacy we'd never had before.

Dad moved in with us for the last five months of his life. Up until that time we had done all we could to keep him in his own home. About three weeks before Dad died, I took time off from work and canceled all my speaking engagements and other appointments. Lo and behold, the world didn't end. People said, "It's okay. You need to be where you need to be." It was a real lesson in humility. You're important, but you're not that important. The world will go on while you do what you need to do.

Getting to know my father and knowing him in new ways helped me understand more about myself.

Being busy, filling every minute with "doing," neglects part of what people need in their lives. We never know what tomorrow is going to bring. I had heard the words for years—people talking about living in the moment—but I didn't understand; I hadn't lived it. Changing the priorities in my life gave me the chance to learn that my dad was really special. I came to understand that he was a deep thinker and a philosopher. Getting to know my father, and to know him so intimately, helped me understand more about myself. Looking back, the illness I had damned for so long had, in truth, offered me a new way to be with my dad. Without his dependency on me and my participation in his care, I might never have experienced or understood what I came to learn. I hope I never forget it.

HERBERT RODGERS

*Although the majority of family caregivers in this country
are women, many men accept the responsibility of primary
caregiver. Herbert Rodgers cares for his wife, Jill, who has
Parkinson's disease, a degenerative spine, and other medical
problems. The couple married young, and Jill's Parkinson's
disease began during the first few months of their marriage.
Jill now needs constant care. When Herbert goes to work,
either Jill's mother or an aide is there to help until he gets
home. Herbert says that through the experience of
caregiving for his wife he has become more sensitive to, and
aware of, the needs of others. "I've had an opportunity to
explore a side of myself that many men don't. I've learned a
lot about expressing my emotions and my feelings." This
sensitivity and vulnerability was evident in my
conversation with Herbert.*

My wife's name is Jill, which means blithe or youthful spirit, and that describes her exactly. She's got a twinkle in her eye; she's my little leprechaun, my little Irishwoman. We laugh a lot. We have to. There are always tears in our situation, but we joke through them. Every once in a while, when the clouds move aside, I get to see her again, the joyful one I married, and that's what keeps me going. It's a peg, an anchor for me.

It's not life as I thought it would be, or planned it in my juvenile thinking; but it's real life, it's deeper than I thought it would be. There's an overall greater goal in my life than making it in business or acquiring material things. You can do all sorts of things in your life out there in the world, but when I walk through the doors of my home I take on the life of my family. There can be tears in my home at any moment of the day, and there often are. Yet, in the midst of the crying, the pain, the falling, and the stitches, there's real joy, and that for me is what I get personally. It's the fulfillment of my life.

It's not life as I thought it would be, or planned it in my juvenile thinking; but it's real life, it's deeper than I thought it would be.

I haven't any need to talk about my care of Jill publicly, but recently the Los Angeles Caregiver Resource Center gave me an award for what they called an inspiring example of devoted and conscientious caregiving. I appreciated it a lot, but I didn't want to make a big deal of it because I'm going to take care of my wife whether anybody sees her or not, behind closed doors or in public. I'm committed to that. But it gave me an opportunity and platform to tell them something about what goes on in our home and what people who are family caregivers have learned. I wrote a little speech about that. Here's the way it went.

"Imagine yourself disabled. Can't? Most of us cannot because we are not. Those who are certainly can. They know what it's like. They know what it's like to wake up in the morning but not be able to get out of bed. They know what it's like to see their clothing hanging in the closet but not be able to put it on. They know what it's like to feel the call of nature but not be able to take themselves to the bathroom. They know what it's like to fall when they try to walk and not be able to protect themselves from being hurt. They know what it's like to drool but not be able to wipe it off without help. They know what it's like to wait and wait and wait. Wait until your caretaker gets you out of bed. Wait until your caretaker dresses you. Wait until your caretaker has time to take you to the bathroom, and then wait until they come back to get you. Continually waiting for someone else because you simply can't do it yourself. Your life is not your own.

I live with a woman who has been progressively disabled by Parkinson's disease for nineteen years, and yet I do not really know how I would handle it if it were me. My wife is the real hero of our family.

So ask yourself, dare I get sick? Dare I become disabled? Who will take care of me? How will I pay for my care? Who can I trust? Will my friends abandon me? Will I be a burden to my friends and family? Will my family stay by me and help me? How will I deal with the guilt of being a burden to everyone? What will happen to my children, my dreams, my plans, and my savings? Will everything I've worked for have to be sold to care for me? Will I be put in some kind of institution if someone will not care for me? Will I have to watch while everything I've worked for dissolves away? Will I have any dignity left when I have another person dress me, feed me, shower me, wipe me? Dare I become disabled?

I live with a woman who has been progressively disabled by Parkinson's disease for nineteen years, and yet I do not really know how I would handle it if it were me. I can only approximate my answers to these tough questions. Ask my wife. She's the real hero of our family."

Our hope, our inspiration, is God. Our faith gives us stability in everything we do. I always tell Jill that we're going to make it, that we're going to go through whatever comes, together. I want her to always know that she's not going to be left. I just reach out and hold her, cradle her, and let her know that it's going to be okay.

JEANNE ZEEB-SCHECTER

This is a story about a mother and a son—not a frail, elderly mother being cared for by a son, but a mother in her early fifties caring for a son diagnosed with AIDS. Jeanne was eager to tell me about her son, Michael, and his partner, Jim, with whom she shared the caregiving experience. Jeanne knows that many parent-child relationships have been shattered by AIDS.

"I know too many people estranged from their living children. I hope my experience will encourage tolerance and understanding in families that have rejected a son who is sick or dying." Through her tears, Jeanne related her experience of pain and personal growth.

We didn't know he had AIDS. My son, Michael, had gone into the hospital with a collapsed and infected lung. His white cell count was extremely low, so the doctors tested his immune system and found he had AIDS. He was told he had about three months to live.

Michael lived another three years after that original diagnosis. During that three-year period I spent about four to five hours every day with Michael. I'd work in the morning, then go to visit Michael and stay until Jim came home. During the last six months of Michael's life, we brought hospice care into the house because my son wanted to die at home. The doctor suggested that the amount of love around him from me, his family, and his partner helped him to live those additional three years. I knew my son really loved me, and I truly loved him.

The course of his illness took me down many different caregiving paths. The first six months of his illness were the hardest for me. I cried, raged, screamed, and yelled. I couldn't find a way to cope even though I felt I knew how to help, both as a mother and a healer. I'm a homeopathic practitioner of complementary medicine, with a specialty in alternative medicine. But Michael resisted my help, which frustrated me since

If you truly love someone, you have to honor what he or she wants to do. It doesn't have to be the way you want it, it doesn't have to make sense to you. You have to love them that much.

he had always bragged about what I did for a living. Yet, he resisted my suggestions about diet, supplements, and homeopathy. I finally got him to try some Chinese formulas to build up his bone marrow, and he was better for a while. But as soon as he found out that it worked, he stopped.

I realized then that my son might not have wanted to live. I believe there was a subconscious part of him that didn't want to be here, and that was the hardest thing for me to accept. Here was my beloved son, the one who'd promised that when I went to an old folks home he'd pull the hairs out of my chin so I didn't look silly. He was going to take care of me and read to me, and now he was the one who was dying. I felt a profound sense of abandonment and betrayal. You're not supposed to lose a child. I experienced constant sadness and grief. I began to see clearly that I needed to learn how to celebrate the life he had, the man he was. I had to get to a spiritual place to give me the perspective I needed to learn. If you truly love someone, you have to honor what he or she wants to do. It doesn't have to be the way you want it, it doesn't have to make sense to you. You have to love them that much.

The time I spent with my dying son was probably the most beautiful and most painful period of my life. We shared an intimacy that, except for my husband, I've never shared with another person. During that time, my biggest challenge as a caregiver was to learn how to be present in the moment, to have no expectations. I spent so many hours with him. We would just hang out together. I'd sit by the bed, read, write, crochet, and watch TV. He'd wake up and look over and go back to sleep. Sometimes we talked for hours. We were totally honest about our deepest feelings. I believe that if someone knows they are going to die, it's important to help them validate the life they've had. Toward the end, Michael and I reviewed his life, and doing that together gave purpose and meaning to a lot of what he had done. It helped me to let go, to be more accepting of the reality of his condition. I had the choice to fall apart or to see how dealing with the death of my child could teach me to become stronger.

The experience of Michael's dying taught me to appreciate the gift of what you have in front of you, instead of crying about what you are not going to have.

The experience of Michael's dying taught me to appreciate the gift of what you have in front of you, instead of crying about what you are not going to have. Just living this moment. And if you truly live that way, you are not losing the person. There was nothing I didn't say. We discussed it all. I don't regret the tragedy of the way he died—how long it was. I feel blessed I had the time with him that I did. Others lose someone in a second. I had this time to be with him. It was truly beautiful.

One night recently, Larry King was interviewing former Los Angeles Dodgers manager Tommy Lasorda who had lost his son at age thirty. Larry King asked him, "How did you get through that? Where is the meaning in the loss of a child?" And Tommy said, "I look at it this way. If God came down and stood in front of me and said, 'Tommy, I've got a deal for you. I'm going to give you this incredible kid. But you'll only have him for thirty years. What do you want to do?' I would do it again." And I agreed.

You have all of these memories of this child and the man he became, and you cannot be sorry for it. I mean, what a gift I had! I am more attentive to those I love now. Life is fragile, and you can lose anyone at any moment. They need to know you love them, and you need to allow them to love you. Let them in. Make time. I was blessed. We had an unconditional love together.

I believe you need to celebrate the life of a loved one who has died. I used to bring Michael sunflowers. He was like sunshine, his face like a sunflower. Once a week I'd bring a new bouquet of sunflowers. He'd beam when I entered the room. So now on his birthday, and also on the anniversary of the evening of his death, we each take a sunflower to the pier at the ocean near where we live. We quietly remember Michael in our own way, and drop our sunflowers into the ocean in memory, in love. It's a celebration of a life, of Michael's life.

JOYCE BIVANS

When I phoned Joyce, she invited me to come to her home.
I accepted her invitation and was delighted to spend the
afternoon in her sunny living room, surrounded by
memorabilia from exotic locations all over the world. Joyce
told me that moving into this modest yet comfortable home
was part of her adjustment to being an "I" after many
years of being a "We." Two years earlier, Joyce's husband
had died. Her work as a marriage and family therapist
and a counselor for family caregivers provides many
opportunities for her to reflect on her personal experience of
caregiving. My encounter with her provided her with
another chance to share her story.

My husband Radcliff—I called him Rad—was a
very healthy person. He ate right, exercised right,
did everything right. Everyone went to Rad for
health information; he was the authority on how to stay
healthy. But there was one thing he didn't do when he had

his annual physical exam, and that was have a colonoscopy. That may have saved his life.

Soon after the diagnosis of colon cancer, Rad had a series of radiation treatments that were very debilitating. After that, we took a vacation and pretended everything was normal. When we returned, we found the cancer had spread to his liver and kidney. My caregiving experience began then; I really became his full-time nurse. Rad was in and out of the hospital seven times in the following months. I wanted to help the person I loved, but it was hard. I was dealing adequately with the practical needs of the moment but not facing the reality of the possibility of my husband's death. People would call and come over, good friends, and they'd say, "Do you want to talk about it?" I would say, "No, there's nothing to talk about," and I'd keep pretending it would all go away.

I wanted to help the person I loved, but it was hard. I was dealing adequately with the practical needs of the moment but not facing the reality of the possibility of my husband's death.

It never really occurred to me that my husband might die. I just kept thinking, "Well, we can see this through." I guess we thought that not thinking about or talking about the possibility of death would keep it away. I never mentioned the possibility of his dying to Rad, and he never mentioned it to me. I just couldn't acknowledge the reality. After Rad died, I read an article about Lauren Bacall and Humphrey Bogart. Bogart was terribly sick with lung cancer, and it was obvious that he was never going to recover. "But we never said a word about it to each other," reflected Bacall. "It was like our secret and if we didn't say it, it wasn't going to be true." When I read that I thought, "Oh sister, and I do mean *sister!*"

One day, Rad went out to get the newspaper. When he came back in the house, he told me he couldn't focus his eyes. The doctor had warned me this would be a symptom that his kidneys had shut down. He never rallied after that. It was fourteen months from diagnosis to death. Rad was only sixty-four.

After Rad's death, I knew I needed help. I got a private trainer to come to my home and help me physically build myself up. I allowed myself to be with people, and I went out with my friends whenever they would ask. I let myself grieve. I believe you have to walk through the middle of the grief because if you hide and try to avoid it, the grief will come on you later in some form of mental or physical pain. I've seen it happen many times. I don't minimize it. I've had painful times and still do. But I think I'm a stronger person, much more compassionate toward others because I've seen my own weaknesses and failures.

I believe you have to walk through the middle of the grief because if you hide and try to avoid it, the grief will come on you later in some form of mental or physical pain.

The first month after Rad died, I didn't believe I could deal with all the details that needed attention. As I look back on our situation, I now feel strongly that unfinished business, financial matters and such, need to be discussed openly and sensibly. Our denial of the reality of Rad's illness left me unprepared. In practical terms, I was left in a mess financially because we never talked about it. I think if Rad had seemed comfortable discussing finances, then I could have as well. One of us needed to break through that wall of denial. Sadly, I've learned these things too late.

I'm learning now how to graciously accept help. I've always felt I should handle everything myself. I'm alone now, and I have to learn to accept help. I've been having some back problems so I'm learning to ask the gardener for help. One thing I understand now is that saying "No, no, no—I can do it myself" to people when they offer help actually shuts out the other person. They want to help, and insisting on being independent and taking care of everything yourself shuts them out.

My adult children tell me now that I never let them know how sick their father was. It was a terrible mistake. It kept our adult children separated from us. I treated them like little children. Had we sat down with them and told them the truth, it would have been a far more meaningful experience for them. They would have come and spent more time with us. I see now how vital it is to bring the adult children in and tell them the truth. If I had it to do over again, I'd be much more forthright about it all. I've learned to talk more openly about my feelings and fears with my children now, and that has helped me grow closer to them. That's been wonderful.

I can tell you another thing I've learned from my experience: caregivers need to take personal time off. I didn't do this, and it was a mistake that took a toll on me. Only a few times would I even let myself go for a walk, and once or twice I'd let myself go to lunch with a friend. I'd come back, and Rad would say, "You're a different person. I see in your face that you had a good time." That's what your loved one wants to see. They don't want to see you beaten down and haggard.

One thing I understand now is that saying "No, no, no—I can do it myself" to people when they offer help actually shuts out the other person.

The thing that's most amazing is that I ran a caregivers' group for years at the center where I worked and also a widows' group. It was my specialty. I was confident that I knew what there was to know about both of those areas. I had read a lot, talked to a lot of people, was interviewed on a national radio broadcast on caregivers, and was well known for running successful caregivers' groups. I guess I was a bit smug. But when I became a caregiver and had to do all the things that people were always telling me they did—cleaning up vomit, changing soiled bed linen, sitting hour after hour waiting for the doctor—for all I thought I knew, I was not prepared for the anger I felt.

I hadn't really understood the anger caregivers feel. As a counselor, I would say things like, "Your anger isn't helping, think how awful it is for your husband, blah, blah, blah." What did I really know? Now I had my own anger, and I'm sure my husband had his. I was angry and ashamed of being angry at the same time. I was mad at my whole situation. What had happened to my life, my plans? We were going to Italy; we had plans to go to Venice on our next vacation. We were financially secure, still young and vital. We had lots of years ahead of us. Our lives were good.

When I counsel clients who are caregivers, I have a real understanding of their anger and where it's coming from. I sincerely believe that a person can grow from these hard experiences.

Now when I counsel clients who are caregivers, I have a real understanding of their anger and where it's coming from. I sincerely believe that a person can grow from these hard experiences. I have seen people shut down, become very bitter, isolate themselves from the world, and let their anger become their over-riding emotion. I was determined not to let that be the path for me. The enormous loss and grief I felt wasn't going to finish my life. I know my husband wouldn't have wanted that for me.

I've found that I'm much more able now to relate to the misfortunes of others. And it's in a deeper way. I'm able to bring a different level of sensitivity and feeling to the work I do. I find that I'm more emotionally available to my clients. I'm just more tuned in to their feelings, I guess. Telling my story has made me a much more effective counselor.

Revealing your personal story is supposed to be a "no-no" for therapists but, in working with family caregivers, I've found it makes a real difference. My clients and I are able to relate on a whole different plane. I have been there. The thing I must always remember is that telling my personal story is for their benefit, not for mine.

It's been two years now since Rad died. I did the best I could, I guess, but I wish I had been able to deal with it more head on. I've certainly experienced some profound personal growth—but, of course, I wish it all hadn't happened. It's hard when you've been part of a "we" to learn to be an "I" again. I'm not the person I was two years ago. I've grown, and I intend to keep growing. There still are lessons I can learn from this experience.

JULIAN MOODY

The recorded phone message on my answering machine was from Julian Moody, who, although eighty-four years old, still worked full time coaching, consulting, advising, and problem solving. "I'm not an authority on their business, but I can help those I advise see how best to solve their problems—little companies, big ones." When we finally spoke, I quickly found out that his work wasn't the reason he had called.

Julian had heard that I was seeking out people who had been caregivers, and he was eager to share his story. Julian invited me to look through the hundreds of photographs he had taken of his wife, Thelma, over the seven-year period he cared for her. "As a tribute to her, I hope to mount a showing in cooperation with the local Alzheimer's group," he told me. "I think it's important for people to see how we loved and valued her even as the disease drained her energy, shrunk her stature, and changed who she was."

My experience as a caregiver started before I was even aware of it. There were little changes taking place in Thelma's behavior for quite a while, but I didn't connect it with dementia at the time. She had macular degeneration, and we both were preoccupied with her eyesight. I guess I thought some of her behavior changes were because of limitations in vision.

She had a habit of playing the piano every afternoon. Then, one day, she just couldn't do it. I thought it was because she couldn't see the sheet music, so I made copies that were very large. They measured eighteen by twenty-four inches. She said she could see it fine but that her hands didn't know what to do anymore. I didn't realize that it was an early stage of deterioration in Thelma's thinking processes.

Once, we went to the supermarket where we'd shopped for thirty years. I left Thelma in the produce department while I went to pick up some other things on our list;

My experience as a caregiver started before I was even aware of it.

when I came back, I couldn't find her. I eventually spotted her wandering around, lost and agitated. I wanted to believe the cause was diminished eyesight, not mental deterioration, but eventually I took her to get some help. One doctor who was good in his diagnosis but extremely poor in his sensitivity sat us both down and blurted out, "Your wife has Alzheimer's."

Over the next few months, Thelma's condition changed rapidly. She became depressed, agitated, nervous—pacing around the house and one day bolting out and running down the street. After that incident, I knew it was time to get some help with her care. There's a wonderful agency here in my town that focuses on the family member doing the caregiving. They sent someone over to help me understand how to manage the changing situation in our household, how to modify my work schedule so I could still keep seeing a few clients, and, most importantly, how to take care of myself. I engaged helpers to come in from nine in the morning until six in the evening. I handled the nighttime alone for a while, but it was too difficult for me. That's when I had another person come in from seven in the evening through six in the morning.

My son helped me organize the running of the household. That freed me up to spend more time with Thelma. Although the Thelma that I used to know wasn't fully there anymore, I wanted her to feel as much like herself as possible. We always dressed her in pretty clothes. We would spend time at the beach because Thelma loved being near the ocean. We'd put her in the wheelchair and take her up into the hills, too. Thelma loved the outdoors.

Although the Thelma that I used to know wasn't fully there anymore, I wanted her to feel as much like herself as possible.

I'd start every day helping the paid caregiver dress and bathe Thelma, and I'd be with her at breakfast and during the morning until Thelma needed a little nap. I was able to keep working almost every day until late in the afternoon. I needed the outside stimulation; it helped me keep balanced. When I came home, Thelma and I would have a little party. We'd sit in the living room and have ice cream and cake. It became our ritual.

Another thing that Thelma and I did together was share a story hour. I had a conversation with a caring and understanding librarian, and she suggested I read to Thelma from books written for ten- to twelve-year-old girls. Some people say that people with Alzheimer's can't focus on a story of any length, but I'm convinced they're wrong. One day, I was reading to Thelma; she was comfortable and relaxed, and I guess I must have been relaxed as well. I don't remember falling asleep, but I do remember waking up and hearing

Thelma say, "And then what happened?" She was still connected to the story.

The Alzheimer's group in town offered a two-day workshop for caregivers. During those two days, there was a session on learning the language of emotions. The leader of the group asked me to think of a time when I was sitting with Thelma: "Tell me what Thelma was saying to you." I told her that just yesterday we had sat together for quite a while, but Thelma didn't communicate anything because she can only use a word or two and they usually don't have anything to do with what is going on right then. "Why don't you describe the expression that was on Thelma's face?" I was able to do that in some detail. Then she asked me to recall what was going on with her hands and feet, and to describe the look in Thelma's eyes and the expression on her brow: "What do you think Thelma was communicating?" I replied, "I guess she was telling me that she was feeling anxious, tense, and uncomfortable." I recalled that I kept asking her, "What do you want, Thelma? More ice cream? A pillow? A blanket? Are you cold? Are you too warm?" There was no answer except more agitated movements of her hands and feet and a rather pained look in her eyes. Now the leader said, "So what if it happens again, how might you handle it differently?" I was silent for a long while. Then I got it. "Oh, I know. I'd just give her a hug." Now, that's a long story about a simple thing. But for a man who is very logical, rational, and linear in the way he thinks, that was a profound learning experience. From that time on, although I didn't

Even as Thelma was growing more distant, I was feeling more deeply what love is. There was a mutual delight in our being together, a kind of spiritual connection, a new feeling of love that I was just beginning to understand. In the midst of all I was losing, I began to know love in a way I had never experienced.

become highly skilled in emotional communication, I began to understand what was going on with Thelma's feelings. I also knew that whatever was going on inside of her, she basically needed to feel safe, secure, and loved.

As things for Thelma changed, my life changed as well. I realized that I was going through a learning process and that this was something that was changing everything in my life. I remember that at one time, when things got difficult, I considered putting Thelma in a care facility and went to look at several. I decided I just couldn't separate from her. I was struggling with the decision, and a friend said to me, "Do you understand what this conflict you're having is all about? You want to have her with you no matter what. Thelma is the heart of your life." And he was right. I needed her as much as she needed me. That remark gave me a new understanding and was a great comfort.

People would tell me all the time how I was such a loving and caring companion, yet it was all very natural to me. Thelma would have done the same thing for me if our situations had been reversed. You know, I really got a lot back from what I gave. It may sound strange, but as I was losing Thelma, I began to understand love in a different way. We so often say the word *love*. We say it so easily without always knowing the feeling of love. Even as Thelma was growing more distant, I was feeling more deeply what love is. There was a mutual delight in our being together, a kind of spiritual connection, a new feeling of love that I was just beginning to understand. In the midst of all I was losing, I began to know love in a way I had never experienced.

LEONARD FELDER

Dr. Leonard Felder is a therapist and a prolific author. Around 1990, when there were almost no other books around offering advice specifically to family caregivers, Dr. Felder's book on the subject came to my attention. The slim volume entitled, When a Loved One is Ill—How to Take Better Care of Your Loved One, Your Family, and Yourself *caught my attention because I had been carrying tremendous guilt about having taken personal time for myself during the period when my mother was fighting ovarian cancer. I desperately needed support and perspective. Several years later, when I began collecting interviews for this book, I managed to schedule a conversation with Dr. Felder. He offers understanding and compassion while reminding family caregivers that it's possible to turn a caregiving crisis into one of the most meaningful and loving times of one's life. The wisdom and advice he shares comes from his personal experience.*

When I was ten years old, my mother found out that she had breast cancer. For the next four years, she went through all kinds of surgery and experienced a dramatic series of emotional ups and downs. This was the most traumatic and powerful experience of my life. I'm still reverberating from how intense it was for me. I've gone through a few similar things—my mother-in-law's leukemia, my brother-in-law's schizophrenia, and another relative's Alzheimer's. Each time has been so intense that I have had to remind myself to slow down and breathe.

When you're a hands-on caregiver, you give up some of your life. I think many caregivers give up too much, and then the task becomes totally consuming. I found that it helped when I got selfish. I'll tell you what I mean. During those periods of my life when I was actively caregiving, I asked myself every day, "What do I need to replenish myself today so I don't feel completely like a victim?" I know you've prob-

I know you've probably heard these words before, but they're really true: "Caregiving is about taking care of yourself so you can take care of others."

ably heard these words before, but they're really true: "Caregiving is about taking care of yourself so you can take care of others." If I've done something for me during the day—whether it's walking or meditating for fifteen minutes, reading something that gives me pleasure, or just taking a hot shower or a relaxing bath—I feel less like a victim. When I've nourished myself, I have something to give.

How do I justify taking this personal time? One time I was flying on an airplane, and the flight attendant gave the best caregiving advice I've ever heard. All of us have heard it, but none of us knew it was caregiving advice. She said, "Put the oxygen mask on your face before helping the person next to you." Most of us would tend to reach out to help the child, the elderly person, the spouse, or whomever was sitting next to us before taking care of ourselves. The reality is that if you don't have adequate oxygen, you can't make good decisions, you get impatient, and you're just not in control. It's a reminder that we need to take care of ourselves first to do our best as caregivers.

For some of us, guilt is always going to be there. We may think, "I shouldn't be doing this. I shouldn't be thinking of myself at a time like this. I should be giving care to the person who's care has been entrusted to me." This may sound strange, but I think it's the good people that feel guilt. People who are insensitive, narcissistic, and indifferent don't experience guilt. Feeling guilt is related to feeling compassion. I truly believe that the guilt a caregiver feels is just part of being a compassionate, feeling, caring, loving person.

I often tell family caregivers, "You're allowed to know your limits." Sometimes the best way to honor your loved one is to know where and when you need to go to get help. Families don't talk about that much. Somehow the expectation is that the primary caregiver can handle whatever challenge comes along. I've found that rarely does anyone let you know it's okay to call in help: a nurse, a respite care person, a social worker, or any other person that can do the things you're not good at. I believe we should do what we're really good at and bring in others to do whatever else may need to be done. For example, there's an art to lifting a person who can't get themselves out of bed. I can't do it. I'm not a weak person, but I can't do it without pulling my back out. I need to know my limitations. Otherwise, I'm going to become the patient. And I'm not going to be a very good caregiver if I'm flat on my back.

I discovered a unique outlet for the pressure and tension that often comes with being a caregiver. I had a friend who let me complain to him once a week. It was a huge relief. I

> *I truly believe that the guilt a caregiver feels is just part of being a compassionate, feeling, caring, loving person.*

urge others to do the same. I suggest finding a complaint partner—someone who will listen to you for ten minutes without interruption—and you return the service by doing the same. Anything and everything that's said during the ten minutes is okay.

My wife and I had another ritual. At the end of the day, we'd say three things that went right that day. I remember one day when my mother-in-law was uncomfortable and the doctors were doing what doctors do, and we couldn't seem to connect constructively with any of them. The day was full of frustrations and worry. When we sat down and searched for our three things for that day, my wife said, "My mom smiled today." I offered, "The nurse that screwed up yesterday didn't today." We were having a hard time coming up with the third one, and then my wife said, "We loaded the dishwasher, ran it, and now we have clean dishes." It makes a difference to experience three things going right, even if 150 things went wrong that day. You build momentum from that, and peace of mind, and hope that tomorrow will be different.

Sometimes the best way to honor your loved one is to know where and when you need to go to get help.

It's interesting to observe how one person in a family often becomes the primary caregiver of a parent or other relative. Very often, a person who's either geographically or emotionally close to the person rushes in to help. The rest of the family empathizes and sympathizes, yet virtually disappears, and the one person who really needs the help and support—the caregiver—gives up asking others to help. The caregiver makes excuses like, "This person is too busy, that one lives too far away, this one has an important job, that one has those little children to take care of."

When I was in that situation I discovered a way to honor the needs of other family members and serve mine as well. I found out that everybody has something they're good at. I'm a good hand-holder. That's what I do best. My sister is good at paperwork. In this way all family members can participate without having the hands-on responsibility for the person needing care.

The need for caregiving often hits people very unexpectedly. And then we who take charge of the caregiving don't think to ask questions of those who have been down this road before. We feel that we have to handle the situation and master everything alone. This attitude is just plain self-destructive, especially when there are organizations like Catholic Family Services, Jewish Family Services, Lutheran Social Services, and so on. These people know so much. They're just waiting for people to call them so they can be of service. For instance, when my mother-in-law was going through chemotherapy, we talked with a woman from a social service agency; she knew where to get shawls to help my mother-in-law feel like a beauti-

The need for caregiving often hits people very unexpectedly. And then we who take charge of the caregiving don't think to ask questions of those who have been down this road before. This attitude is just plain self-destructive.

ful woman when she didn't have any hair, where to get papaya drinks to calm her nausea, and where to get protein powder to help her get strong. They know how to deal with these kinds of things, and what to do when doctors have three different opinions, and how to handle financial confusion. There are people out there to help you and support you in these ways. But first, we have to break out of our shame or denial and share some of the problems (the so-called "dirty laundry") with someone who's a stranger.

In spite of the problems and pressures, there can be great personal rewards in caregiving. People don't always realize how much intimacy and closeness is possible. Just holding my mother's hand and feeling the connection between us was a very special thing. Some people may not have a good relationship with a parent, but when their parent becomes ill, the personality traits that caused conflict fade into the background, and they can connect with the essence, warmth, neediness, and spirit of the parent. Lots of times, I think, personality gets tossed aside by the illness and you have a chance to connect with this person on a soulful or spiritual level, perhaps for the first time. It can be, I believe, one of the richest experiences in their life and in yours.

My mother-in-law, an anxious, agitated person for her whole life, was, in the last weeks of her life, open to being loved. And there was such warmth and connection. The day before she died, I just sat there and held her hand. This is something I never would have done before. She had never been open to that kind of thing, yet now she seemed to welcome it. If there's a situation like this in your life and if you have some way of connecting in a deeper way or a more conscious way, then I say grab it. It's something you'll remember for the rest of your life.

In spite of the problems and pressures, there can be great personal rewards in caregiving. People don't always realize how much intimacy and closeness is possible.

When you've been through this with someone, you really know how fragile we are. When you start to appreciate how much in your body is working right, you start to truly appreciate the miracle of human life. And you start to realize what's really important. Caregiving gave me an opportunity to clarify what I want to devote my life to. I knew I didn't want to waste my life in a career that meant nothing, so having a personal life and work that gave me deep satisfaction and a sense of being of value to others became a high priority. It was through my caregiving experiences that I gained this perspective.

There are gifts to be found through the caregiving experience even when the focus is on bathing someone, wiping a bottom, making a trip to the doctor, or doing one of a million different tasks of immediate priority. Even if you're enduring someone's violent outburst or experiencing their depression or unresponsiveness, there are ways to look for the grace in the experience of being a caregiver.

Caregiving is a great time to dig deep and find your Higher Power, your God, your faith. Many people use their spiritual energy to beg for a cure, but don't blame God if it doesn't happen. This spiritual energy could more constructively be put into prayers that ask, "Please give me the strength to be open to the possibilities of connection and to people who can help; to surround myself with people who are positive, warm, and loving; and to help me to learn from this experience."

LIZ AND DAVE KRUGER

I arrived at Liz and Dave's home just as some friends who had joined them for Sunday night supper were leaving. Liz and Dave had explained to me beforehand that their lives were too busy, their energy too committed to family matters, for them to make time during the day for a lengthy appointment. They had suggested I come over in the evening after their daughters had gone to bed. It was the end of a long day, but somehow Liz and Dave pulled together the energy to tell me their story. They have three daughters. Two are normal girls in their teens. Their youngest daughter, Shoshi, who just turned eleven, has a rare neurological disorder called Rett Syndrome. Our conversation revealed a story of deep love, dedication, and commitment. Because Liz and Dave's opinions and answers to my questions were similar, I've combined them here into a single voice.

You've got your life and a family, and then something unexpected hits and all of the pieces fall to the ground like children's blocks. We knew quite early on that something was not right, but even the most experienced doctors hadn't suspected Rett Syndrome, because it is so rare. Finally, one neurologist diagnosed Shoshi as having Rett Syndrome and said, "I'm so sorry to tell you that this child will not live past ten, you will not be able to take care of her, she will self-mutilate," and on and on. This doctor turned our world upside down.

Kids with Rett Syndrome are born seemingly normal, but between the ages of one and two they lose skills they've just begun to develop, like speech, the ability to walk, and other motor and coordination skills. Shoshi first lost the use of her hand and developed a movement that looked like handwashing or clapping. She has a hand-to-mouth movement that she can't stop. It's repetitive and constant. Her major handicap is the lack of motor skills. For example, Shoshi may want to look left and will look right instead. Many who have Rett Syndrome cry in terror night after night. When Shoshi screamed through the night, we couldn't find anything to soothe her. It was very, very difficult.

You've got your life and a family, and then something unexpected hits and all of the pieces fall to the ground like children's blocks.

We've always taken care of Shoshi at home. Shoshi goes to a special school that can handle her needs for total care. In the summer, she goes to a camp program. Years ago, there would have been no way for us to do this. We're fortunate to live in a county that has many services, many agencies to deal with all kinds of special needs. We're so grateful to be in touch with all the advantages and services around us. We live in a dense, well-to-do metropolitan area, but if we were in a rural setting we'd have far fewer advantages and services available to us. Still, we're constantly challenged to find the right education and therapy.

You ask what Shoshi can do. She can smile, hug, walk, eat if fed, and listen to us when we read or tell a story—but she's passive. We try to understand what it must be like for her, not being able to communicate or use her hands, not being able to say she is cold or hungry or in pain. If it were us, we'd just close up shop and check out of this world. What would be the point? Yet, despite all that she lives with, Shoshi keeps plugging along. She doesn't give up. A few weeks ago we were in the hospital with her, and although she was drugged, she was strong and fighting to come back to her world. Her desire to belong in this world is very strong. She gives us the message that she not only wants to belong but has something to contribute. And that very often drives us. If she is willing to push, who are we to give up?

Our world has caved in. To deal with this we need to pick up and build a new world.

We believe that Shoshi and other children with Rett Syndrome know and understand more than they can express, but measuring IQ is impossible. Neurologists claim that Rett Syndrome is a developmental disorder, and that once certain skills are lost, the deterioration will plateau. In our experience, this isn't so. Shoshi had seizures last week, and things seemed to get worse. Her medical issues are becoming more severe and pronounced. Things don't get better or even stay the same for Shoshi. It's been heartbreaking to watch our daughter progressively lose skills. This is something that we continually deal with. Our world has caved in. To deal with this, we need to pick up and build a new world.

We've learned a huge amount about patience, pacing, and the wonderful gift of time. When we're with Shoshi, it is like being in a timeless zone. Last spring we went walking in a garden. We debated about letting her walk or not. We decided it didn't matter how long it took. So we walked, and she got tired and sat down on the pavement and just gazed and seemed delighted. We started talking about how we schedule ourselves—you know, first we need to see this and then that and then go over there and not miss that. It was Shoshi who reminded us to just step back and enjoy the moment. She looked at the garden for a while and then fell asleep, and we had to just sit there. What a gift not to have a schedule, not to even look at a watch. Time didn't matter. We observed other families running around, and we sat there and thought, this is such peace. We could look at the situation one way and say how sad it is, but we've learned to look at it all another way and see the gift.

We appreciate what we have so much more. Things like speech. We've become more conscious of the words that we speak, to weigh them and consider the impact of what is said. Shoshi cannot speak at all, and there are times when we who have the gift of speech are guilty of misusing it.

We could look at the situation one way and say how sad it is, but we've learned to look at it all another way and see the gift.

What we learn from Shoshi is that this gift is not to be abused. We thought about that recently when the spring was very wet and the water table was high, and our back yard and the yards of our neighbors were swamped. Some ugly, nasty language was exchanged between neighbors who blamed one another for the mud and mess. We are given the ability to speak, and we should not abuse it. It's a lesson we've learned from someone who can't speak.

There are gifts that Shoshi is able to give to others at her school. In kindergarten, a troublemaker boy for some reason took a liking to Shoshi. The teacher decided to use Shoshi to modify his behavior. She told the boy that if he didn't hit anyone and if he did his assignment, he could have ten special minutes with Shoshi. And by gosh, he did his work and behaved. I guess he really wanted to be with her. Shoshi turned this kid into a kinder soul. And it goes on. A group of teens helps us out on some weekends and evenings. A few of these kids are thinking about careers in special education based on their connection with Shoshi. Something about her gives a special meaning to people. It's profound. She teaches without words. Her spirit speaks loudly.

Shoshi attends a summer camp that has a program for kids with special needs. One year, Liz was a music teacher there. One little boy at the camp caught my eye—a sweet kid, a gentle soul. Every morning he chose to be with Shoshi. He wanted to push her stroller. He seemed to enjoy being with her so much. When he finally made the connection that Liz was her mother, he said, "Oh, you're Shoshi's mom. You are so lucky!" That took us completely by surprise. Usually, from adults we hear Shoshi is lucky to have us. Yet, somehow, kids are happy to be with her. We marvel at this.

One of the hardest things about being a parent to a handicapped child is trying to maintain a normal life for the others in the family.

Shoshi is not predictable. She can turn from a sunny day into a storm within the space of five minutes. Recently we went to a relative's house, and Shoshi was very vocal and loud. Another family was visiting as well, and when we walked in everyone stopped and stared. You get used to these stares. What do you do? For some reason we said, "Shoshi likes to make a good first impression." Everyone laughed, and it dispelled the whole thing. You've got to have a sense of humor.

One of the hardest things about being a parent to a handicapped child is trying to maintain a normal life for the others in the family. We're a team, a unit. It's important for us to give the message to our other girls that they are special, too. We have three girls, and we believe that our energy as parents should be divided equally among each. It's always a little less sleep and little more pushing to fit it all in. But no matter how preoccupied we get, we don't forget about the other kids. I recall one time last year when our daughter Chava asked if her mother could lead the girls' choir in her school. Our first response was to say, of course not, there isn't time to do that. But the second response was, how could we possibly say no? It wouldn't be fair. If our daughter Nomi is playing in a basketball game, for instance, we might not want to pack Shoshi up and make the effort to attend, but we know we must do it for Nomi.

When we talk to families whose child has been diagnosed with Rett Syndrome, we suggest they take it a step at a time. It can bring tears to your eyes when you get off the phone. But you can't say much to the new families. You listen, you answer questions; but they'll have to learn the insights and lessons for themselves. It doesn't seem right to tell them what may be down the path. Look at "now," we say. The point is, you plan for the future, but you live one day at a time. It gets you through. When we have a good day with Shoshi, we feel enormous gratitude.

You plan for the future, but you live one day at a time.

With a handicapped child there's no finality; the bad times don't end, it's a continual process. For us there's always deep, deep sorrow and often anger, and we suffer endless grief. You can be doing something like driving or shopping, and all of a sudden you feel hot tears behind your eyes. And sometimes we get mad at God. God is supposed to be compassionate, the healer of the sick. Yet, Shoshi elicits compassion in others. So maybe that's how we should interpret God—as a God of compassion.

For a young girl who has had so many things taken away from her, Shoshi shows a resilience that is special and rare. When we look at her, we can't help but marvel at the power of a smile! She can look right into your soul. We sense what she's thinking much of the time, but sometimes we can't and we'll say, "Shoshi, we know you're telling us something, but we just don't understand." She's the patient one. She'll wait until we catch on.

We know we don't get enough sleep or physical exercise, and the emotional strain is constant. But we're blessed with many special friends who are part of our journey and our lives. We're always there for each other, and that's enormously important. We hear many times of families who find support from their religion, but at this time we struggle with what that really means for us. We find strength from our other two daughters, and curiously, strength from Shoshi as well.

There are many comforting thoughts in Rabbi Kushner's book, *When Bad Things Happen to Good People*, such as the notion that through people like Shoshi a godliness comes as a gift to all of us. But we'd trade it in a heartbeat for a little girl who could braid her own hair and do normal things. We often wonder at whose expense these lessons are being taught. Perhaps someday we'll understand. But we believe there are more compassionate ways to learn these lessons that are not so rough and tough on her.

We've shared with you the God-wrestling that we constantly go through, yet we want you to know that for us Shoshi is a bundle of love. We're both very proud of her. We like to take her places, even though every time we take her somewhere people stare. Sometimes things like this can pull families apart. Not us. We know we're in this together for the long haul.

LOIS SACKS

*The U.S. census tells us there are 76 million baby boomers.
Many of these baby boomers are involved with caring for
an elderly and frail parent—a parent who often lives far
away. Long-distance caregiving presents many logistical
challenges. Sometimes adult children make the decision to
move closer to the parent; often, the more practical solution
is to move the parent closer to the adult children. Either
situation results in compromise, adjustments, and
transitions. In addition to logistics, there are emotional
challenges. Old resentments, suppressed anger, feelings of
childhood deprivation, and unacknowledged needs can add
to the stress of the situation. Lois Sacks will tell you that it's
never too late to heal old hurts. We talked about this one
day as I sat in her charming kitchen in a wooded
residential area close to Washington, D.C. Our
conversation was about healing, not of the body but of the
relationship between parent and child.*

M y parents lived in Florida. My husband and I lived in Maryland. After my father died from cancer, my mother spent her time with her friends and her card games, and things seemed to be going normally. Then she developed uterine cancer. Even though it was a large tumor, the prognosis after surgery was good. But after about two years, they found a spot on her lung. The cancer had spread. She was sick, living alone in Florida, and many of her friends had either died or were moving away. I kept going back and forth to Florida to check on how she was doing. The stress and the constant travel exhausted me. One day, I realized this arrangement just wasn't going to work. My husband and I began having conversations about the possibility of my mother moving closer to us.

I had spent a lifetime wanting a better relationship with my mother, but I had no clue how to fix it.

I had always had a very difficult relationship with my mother. I could barely stand to be with her even one or two nights, and here I was thinking about bringing her to live close to me. I had spent a lifetime wanting a better relationship with my mother, but I had no clue how to fix it. We just couldn't communicate. As a child, I once blurted out, "You never tell me you love me!" And she said, "That's not how we do it. I don't have to say it. Of course I love you." During my adolescence, our conversations became irrelevant or contentious. I left home, went to college, married, and embarked on raising my own family. Living in another city, I maintained a cordial but rather superficial relationship with my mother. Now the state of her health was changing everything.

My brothers were angry about the plan to move Mother. They couldn't believe I wanted to take her away from her friends and from where she had made her home in her retirement. However, they weren't the ones that were making the constant trips to Florida. That seemed to be the role of the only daughter. Also, I guess I secretly hoped that, living close to my mother, there might be a chance to work on a relationship that had disintegrated, or maybe one that never really existed. I was hoping that this could be a chance to know this woman who I had, for so much of my life, absolutely resented and certainly didn't understand. That, in fact, is exactly what happened.

I asked my mother how she felt about moving, and she almost immediately agreed that it would be good living close to us. I looked for independent living situations near where I lived and found a great place she liked. To my surprise, she made immediate plans to move, and in one month Mother arrived, ready to set up a new life for herself. At seventy-eight, she was a very independent woman; she made friends easily and played cards every day.

After a time, we found that the cancer had spread more extensively. She trusted my husband and me to do the right thing for her. Like families often do in the face of a terminal disease, we desperately searched for a medical miracle to cure her cancer. But what happened was a healing instead of a cure—a healing of the relationship between my mother and myself. The time she was with us gave me a chance to know a different mother, and she took the opportunity to finally get to know her daughter. Not until I became her caregiver did I realize how needy we both were for each other. Building a genuine relationship with my mom during the two years she lived here was the mutual gift that grew from my sharing what life she had left and then participating in her dying.

Like families often do in the face of a terminal disease, we desperately searched for a medical miracle to cure her cancer. But what happened was a healing instead of a cure—a healing of the relationship between my mother and myself.

I began to see another side of my mother. She knew the prognosis was not good, but she went through it all with a smile on her face. I saw her resiliency as she scarcely shed a tear over what she had left behind or what lay ahead. She poured herself into doing whatever she could to survive, and she did it with amazing style and grace. My mother showed me what it meant to truly live in the face of death.

I remember being amazed when, shortly after her arrival, I took her shopping for a winter coat. No basic black utilitarian number for her; she selected a bright red wool coat with a smashing black velvet beret. And each time she wore it, whether to a grueling chemotherapy treatment or someplace more pleasant, she lit up with a special *joie de vivre* that blew me away. I've kept that coat and have worn it each winter since she died. Each time I put it on, it's as if she has her arms around me giving me that warm hug I always craved.

My mother showed me what it meant to truly live in the face of death.

Even when the red coat was out of season, she somehow remained cloaked in unfathomable optimism. She made new friends, took advantage of nearly every excursion offered at her new residence, and kept herself looking beautiful at all times. Our trip to buy a wig, in anticipation that she would lose her hair as a result of chemotherapy, was colored by her sense of adventure in finding a new hairdo, not the dread of what was to come. I was on the verge of tears at the horror of what she, who was always so concerned about her appearance, would have to face. Yet, she joked with the saleswoman and gently tried to prod me into considering a wig for myself so I wouldn't have to be bothered with my unruly natural curls in the summer humidity. It was a brave display of humor and courage.

The bleakness of her prognosis did not interfere with her determination to go on living for as long as she could. She who loved to shop tuned into cable TV shopping when she could no longer manage the shopping trips, or she'd thumb through catalogs and order herself occasional gifts. If her phone didn't ring, she simply picked it up and called me or someone else she knew to make plans. Her conversations were cheerful and upbeat. Even when she began to have periods of disorientation, she was aware of what was happening and could even laugh about them.

As her disabilities increased and she became less and less able to carry on independently, she gratefully and graciously welcomed the opportunity to have shifts of hired caretakers help her remain in her own apartment. They too became her friends, inspired by her quiet courage and her refusal to complain. I got to see a resilience that I never knew my mother possessed.

When Mother was weak and tired, we would often sit together. Quiet was okay. Doing nothing was okay. Just being there, being quiet with her, was healing. I learned about silence, about not needing to be doing something all the time. That was a special lesson that I was privileged to have learned, and I treasure it. She had a zest for life, and even in her illness she taught me how to take each day as a gift and simply live it, enjoy it. We never talked about what had happened to our relationship in the past. We just let it grow and change, and we both sensed a mutual acceptance emerging—and love. We really got to know who each of us were, and we both really enjoyed every minute of our new relationship.

We never had those heart-to-heart talks on the meaning of life that I so often thought I craved, but each time we greeted and parted, our hugs got tighter and longer. Early on I had begun saying to her "I love you," and she immediately

Just being there, being quiet with her, was healing. I learned about silence, about not needing to be doing something all the time.

responded in kind—something I had desperately wanted to hear as a child. We exchanged those words in every phone call and every visit thereafter. They sustained both of us, and a connection I had never before felt grew and thrived. When she died in my arms, I whispered, "I love you," and I knew that she had heard me when it mattered—and I had heard her, too.

The whole experience was like a gift. Often, you hear of people working so hard to heal rifts and misunderstandings between mother and daughter. Our situation was quite different. Just letting go of the old stuff allowed our transformation to happen. Suddenly she became a beautiful person, and I truly appreciated her. We began to enjoy every single moment we spent. It was very precious.

I recall thinking that this horrible disease is killing my mother and yet it's giving us a gift we never would have had.

Maybe we always have the opportunity to see things differently, but we just don't see it. Maybe a sense of urgency, when time is short, suddenly allows something like this to happen. I recall thinking that this horrible disease is killing my mother and yet it's giving us a gift we never would have had.

Her dying was profoundly moving and unforgettable. My children got to see their grandmother die with dignity and a sense of integrity. When she died, I felt a warmth and peacefulness envelop me. It was uplifting and wonderful to actually be there with her. I never would have believed it. I think the greatest gift, my legacy, was that my negative, unconstructive relationship with my mother had been healed. I miss her still, so very much. She's very much alive to me in so many ways. It is a magical, mystical connection that I treasure.

The experience with my mother has also enriched my relationship with my husband. Since her death, we've reorganized our priorities, slowed down together. We value our lives in a new way. We've really worked at it. I'm an attorney, mainly in family law issues, and that keeps me extremely busy. I've recently made considerable changes and have begun to re-nurture myself. I'm working on saying no to taking on more work, and my husband is doing the same. My husband has become a more well-rounded person who wants to grab life and experience it now, in the slow lane, not the fast lane. It's not been an easy transition, but we're doing it. It is amazing to see the changes in both of us that I would have thought were impossible. We're learning not to let life run by us.

The experience with my mother started me on a new path. Suddenly her life ended, and it hit me. When you personally experience it, you get it. It's ironic that we learn more about life by learning about death, but I think that is true— it's the real learning. For me, nothing will ever take that away.

MARTHA SANCHEZ

A mailing for a day-long seminar sponsored by the Los Angeles Caregivers Resource Center indicated the speakers would be family caregivers. Of course, that was of interest to me, so I registered for the event. The first speaker was Martha Sanchez. The Los Angeles Caregivers Resource Center provides family caregivers with referrals, personal advice, and other types of assistance. When Martha left her husband, the agency helped her locate services for her paralyzed adult daughter, Janice, and provided counseling as Martha's personal situation and Janice's care needs changed. Martha told her story to an attentive audience; it gave others hope and inspiration. I think her story, briefly retold here, will inspire you as well.

I have three children. My son Daniel is twelve years old, my daughter Sara is fourteen, and my daughter Janice just turned thirty. In December of 1997, Janice was injured in a car accident. She suffered severe head trauma that has left her non-verbal, non-communicative, and non-ambulatory. That was the beginning of our new way of life. I tried to make it all work—caring for the younger children, becoming a full-time caregiver for Janice, and holding up my end of the marriage. Janice's dependent condition had a great impact on a family that was already having difficulties. Eventually I separated from my husband, and I've now filed for divorce.

I have a huge family. Unfortunately, and incomprehensibly so to me, not one member of my family could bear to be with Janice after the accident. Some of them came once to the hospital, and even that was too much. It was easier for them to pretend that Janice and I didn't exist anymore. That was very painful for me. My mother did try to help, but she treated Janice like a two-year-old. My mother felt that's what you do. When Janice would do something out of her control, my mother would scold her. And then we'd all be upset. She

I'm an around-the-clock caregiver, and it's an adjustment every single day.

didn't understand; it was causing too much stress. Finally she stopped coming. My husband's family kept telling me to put Janice in a home. They said that she'd gotten herself into the accident and we shouldn't spend our lives taking care of her. The tension in our house was terrible. When my husband came home, Jan and I went into her room and just stayed there. That was the beginning of my realization that things had to change.

Now we've moved out from living with my husband, and I can function without worrying about his reactions. I'm free to spend the time I need to care for Jan. This might seem like a small thing, but for me it's a new life, a new world. It's a sad thing that I have to handle all this alone. I'm an around-the-clock caregiver, and it's an adjustment every single day. We don't know what the day will bring. It's very different than other mothers and daughters. Jan has to communicate with her eyes to me. That we've learned together to communicate this way is the greatest joy. Jan doesn't have words to use, so I've learned other ways of reaching out to understand what she is feeling. I've been putting energy into improving my communication with each of my other children, spending time with them, even if it's for short periods when I don't need to be with Janice. I share their lives in new ways. I've learned how to be a silent support for Jan and be there for my other children, too. In a way, Janice has blessed us all with a different learning. Yes, this way we live now is a different life. We have a partnership, Jan and I, and I've come to realize that I have a friend.

Being a caregiver has taught me to have little goals—a one-day-at-a-time philosophy. I've learned from Janice about patience, about reaching out of myself to others. For a long time, I only had tears of sadness. Now, although I can't really explain it to you, they are tears of joy. I've made a decision. No matter what, my Jan is alive and every day is a celebration of life. I stop and realize what beauty there is in life and then look at the challenges we have and what it's going to take. I know I can find ways to help myself, to care for Jan and Sara and Daniel, too. You do have to be realistic. At some point, you reach a stage of reality and are no longer hoping for full recovery, expecting a miracle. I think then you begin to set reasonable goals. Each day gives you strength and courage, and each day brings you blessings. Joy is when I see my Jan smile. It's simple things that are my hope and strength. Just today is enough for me.

Joy is when I see my Jan smile. It's simple things that are my hope and strength.

This change in my life, becoming a caregiver for Jan, has brought me a gift—a gift of self-confidence, love, and appreciation, despite the obstacles that will continue to face us. A professor of mine once told me that we have a choice: Why not open the windows of your mind and let the sun and the warmth and the love come in? It's about choices. It's about what we do with what we've got to deal with. I'm not letting anger or bitterness or sadness or depression overwhelm me and overtake my heart. That would really be a tragedy. So when I have occasional feelings of sadness or despair, I work hard to have that negative energy become a positive thing. It's like a miracle that has happened to my life. Maybe I can inspire other caregivers, and they will see they too have strength.

MARY CARLSON

Mary Carlson is retired and lives alone. She was widowed at a very young age, raised her family, and has generally led a life she'd label ordinary. Mary volunteers for a local hospice group and has discovered that there's nothing "ordinary" about the caring visits she makes to those who are sick and dying. There are volunteer caregivers in big cities and small towns all over our country. Each volunteer has his or her own reasons for doing this work; each has his or her own individual experiences to share. Mary can only tell her own story, but the rewards she finds in visiting the sick and dying aren't so different from those found by other volunteers. Mary is soft-spoken, modest, and friendly. She was seventy-two years old at the time of this interview. Our conversation began with her telling me a little about her younger years.

At the age of thirty-six, I had two children and was expecting a third. That summer my husband wasn't feeling at all well. One doctor said it was ulcers, but another suspected stomach cancer, and that's what it turned out to be. First they gave him cobalt treatments to shrink the tumors, and then they operated. They knew he wasn't going to make it after that. He came home from the hospital, and for the short time he lived I took care of him. My sister came out from New Jersey to help me with the three children. (I'd had the baby by then.) Without my sister, I couldn't have managed. The day after I came out of the hospital after having the baby, my husband went back in, and they tried chemotherapy. That treatment was very new then. They knew he wouldn't make it, but they were determined to try everything. He was so young when he died.

Some months later, I went to work in the same hospital as a volunteer. I wanted to be able to walk by the hospital and not

Hospice isn't about medicine, hospice is about caring.

feel lost and sad. To start healing myself, I made myself go into the room that my husband had been in. After a couple of years, I gave up the volunteering because I had to go back to work. It took me a long time to know that I could go on, to understand that I could find ways to have happiness in my life.

I was a teacher for many years, then I worked at the post office before taking retirement. That's when the work I'm doing now began. I started working with hospice. A friend of mine, a nurse, told me they needed volunteers badly. I told her I didn't know anything about medicine. And she told me, "Hospice isn't about medicine, hospice is about caring."

I went through the hospice training course, and one day I got a phone call and was asked if I'd like to visit an older woman who was dying of breast cancer. They needed someone just to sit and visit with her a few times a week. I rang her doorbell, went in, sat down, and then realized I really didn't know what to do or say. Finally I said, "Look, if you want to talk, I'd be happy to have a conversation with you. If you don't feel like talking, let me sit here and just be with you, okay?" We shared both silent times and deep conversations, and in the months before she passed away, we became friends. During the years I've worked with hospice, I have made friends with many people who were dying. That's what hospice volunteers do.

One time, I was assigned a lady in her mid-fifties who was dying of colon cancer. The doctor said she probably wouldn't live more than six months. On my first visit, I didn't like her much. She was so angry that she was dying that talking with her was almost impossible. She was more difficult to be with than anyone I had ever visited before. The miracle was that we eventually became as close as sisters. We were of different religions, different life-styles and very different temperaments. Yet, our relationship worked for some reason. I don't have patience in many situations, but in this circumstance and in so many other hospice visits I've made over the years, I seemed to have endless patience.

What I discovered in my hospice work was that I can give many who are ill and dying what they need, and it doesn't take anything away from me. Actually, my contact with them gives me back more than I give.

We talked about everything. She told me about her past—her husband, her family, her experiences. And we laughed together a lot. I spent a lot of time at her house, and the relationship we developed was wonderful. I know I gave her a great deal as a friend, and I got a great deal back: warmth, love, and appreciation, from both her and her husband. Her husband couldn't handle her illness and periodically had to leave for three or four days. I moved in when he was gone. She lasted a year and a half, much longer than the doctors predicted. I was with her when she died. She was a special person.

What I discovered in my hospice work was that I can give many who are ill and dying what they need, and it doesn't take anything away from me. So many of these people have hard struggles. Some are paralyzed; others can't talk or feed themselves. My visits give them some happiness, and actually, my contact with them gives me back more than I give. People tell me that they could never be with people who are dying, and they wonder how I do this work. But for me, each person I get to know is a special and rewarding experience.

I'm doing something I didn't know I could do, and I'm really doing it well. I sincerely feel love for each person I get to know in my hospice visits. I tell them that they're loved, that they're cared for. When one of my new friends dies, I know that I've made a real difference in their last days. I guess what I do is help people die. I don't mean that in a bad way. What I'm saying is that I make their dying easier for them and their last days less lonely. When my time comes, I hope I have a hospice volunteer like me around.

NAN KAUFMAN

I arrived at Nan Kaufman's suburban home just in time for our appointment. I didn't know her, hadn't even spoken with her on the telephone. A mutual friend had made the contact, and the message I received was that Nan was eager to talk with me. At that time, I was scheduling conversations with parents who were caregivers for children with special needs. I was delighted for the opportunity to speak with her, and most appreciative that she was so willing to talk with me. Nan was generous, not only with her hospitality but also in sharing with me, and with you, her heartfelt and deeply touching story.

Being a caregiver is the way I define myself and my life for better or for worse, no matter what other roles I play. I'm a psychotherapist, which is work that I love, and I'm a wife, a friend, a daughter, and a sister; but what really defines almost every moment for me is being a mom. My older son, Jason—we call him Jay—is seventeen;

my younger, Aaron, is fourteen. Both boys have cerebral palsy.

Our older son is severely disabled. He uses a wheelchair and doesn't have the use of his hands. Although Jay's speech has been affected, we can understand him most of the time. There was a time when we thought he would not talk at all. Now he speaks nonstop. He is delightful and sweet and funny. My youngest son is mildly affected. He uses crutches and has impairments, but not like my older son.

Cerebral palsy is an umbrella description for a group of disorders related to muscle and movement control, visual disorders, seizures, and various sensory disabilities believed to originate in the brain. There's not one specific cause of cerebral palsy. At one time, it was believed that cerebral palsy resulted from injury to the brain before, during, or immediately after birth. New theories suggest other possible causes, such as abnormal brain development, insufficient circulation to areas of the brain, an infection in the brain, or bleeding in the brain. Whatever the cause, this is what we live with.

Being a caregiver is the way I define myself and my life for better or for worse, no matter what other roles I play.

Jay was born two months premature, but we were told he was fine. It was the end of October. The weather was very cold, and I was told to keep him in. He cried constantly. I was a new mom, and I felt inadequate to parent a child who was so miserable. The baby would cry, and then I would cry. I couldn't soothe him, and everyone was giving me advice. A friend of mine had a child at about the same time, and her perfect little baby never cried. It was not a good feeling to be unable to comfort my child. If there had been a diagnosis, it would have been easier. But it was nine months before the doctor finally told us that Jay had cerebral palsy.

With no family history of cerebral palsy, we dared to get pregnant again. It was devastating to find out Aaron also had cerebral palsy. Thankfully, he was not as severely affected. I dove headfirst into the care of the boys, even though I was depressed and had no time to heal. I had so much to do and adjust to. It's gotten easier as the boys have gotten older. The demands are different, and I've discovered more about how to take care of myself. I know that's the bottom line for any caregiver: to take care of yourself so you can care for others. It's hard to remember that.

Something I've learned along the way is not to judge the choices other people make. It is a hard thing to do. We're all raised in some ways to be judgmental, but I've learned now not to judge anyone else's choices. For example, so many people ask me why I didn't put my boys in an institution. For some people, that might be the choice they would need to make; it might be right for them. But it never occurred to us to do anything but have them at home.

Something I've learned along the way is not to judge the choices other people make.

I'm well aware that some marriages risk falling apart under the stress of having children with special needs. Our marriage has, thankfully, survived the strain. Through the years, we've grown into our individual roles, though it hasn't been easy. My husband and I are able to talk now about how, at one time, he wished he could escape. And I can tell him about the many times I've wanted to run away, too. We've sheltered each other. He'd drive by a park and see some father throwing a ball to his son, and it would hurt, but he wouldn't tell me how miserable that made him feel because he didn't want to hurt me more. And I did the same. I'd keep quiet about my feelings. For a while, I resented my husband for not being more involved. Now I've learned to ask him for help in a way he can hear. It's been uneven for us. We haven't always been able to be mutually supportive.

We're fortunate to have very loving and supportive families. Both sets of grandparents have been phenomenal. My husband's parents have embraced the boys and been an amazing part of their lives. And one of my father's great joys was spending time with the boys as well. I have a photo album of him with the boys, and they are laughing in all of the pictures. You never knew he was dealing with children with special needs. Some families aren't there for them. We are very blessed.

You cannot be down around these kids because they aren't. They are so upbeat. The older one always has pain, and yet he doesn't complain. Jay will say, "My head itches" or "My eye itches." I am constantly struck by what it must be like not to be able to rub your eye. I am always faced with what these children can't do—what we take for granted. And it helps me be patient with them, even though it puts constant demands on me. Yet,

No matter how lousy my day has been, when I look at these children at the end of the day, I can't help but put all my little stuff in a petty category and embrace a healthy life perspective.

no matter how lousy my day has been, when I look at these children at the end of the day, I can't help but put all my little stuff in a petty category and embrace a healthy life perspective.

Neither one of the boys defines himself as disabled, which is fascinating to us. They are aware of their disabilities, but that is not their first definition of themselves. One day, we were visiting a radio station and hanging out with the disc jockey. It was great fun. About a week later, Aaron called up to request a song and said, "Hi, we were there a few weeks ago." And he went on to describe his hair color and other things that would identify him, but he never said they were the kids with the wheelchair and the walker. That's not how he describes himself or his brother.

One day, I was driving Jason to a recreation program, and he yakked so much I could hardly concentrate on driving. We pulled up, and I was thinking that I desperately needed some quiet time. There was another boy in the car next to us wearing an oxygen mask. I thought, "Thank you, God. Thank you for that reminder." Life has handed me a number of these kinds of experiences. I took Aaron to a therapist one day, and I was sitting in the waiting room next to the receptionist. As the receptionist tried to schedule an appointment with another client, I overheard the client say, "No, I can't come that day. That's the day I have my chemotherapy." Again, "Thank you, God."

It is scary to contemplate that I'll be caregiving for my entire life. Knowing this has made me more conscious of my health. I owe it to my children to be as healthy as I can be.

Because of my children, I have grown enormously. But this is not growth anyone would go looking for. This is not something you choose. The growth has been painful and difficult, and yet it has given me an amazing perspective on life. It is scary to contemplate that I'll be caregiving for my entire life. Knowing this has made me more conscious of my health. I owe it to my children to be as healthy as I can be. We don't know what the future holds. Yet, we know that in our lifetime we will always be caregivers.

It is easier seventeen years later, but there are moments and situations arising all the time that are difficult. It's still one day at a time. It is a life lesson. How else is there to really live? None of us knows what will be.

Caregivers need to feel free and comfortable to express their feelings. You need to find someone to whom you can say, "At this moment, I hate this. I hate my kid. I hate my husband." You don't want to stay stuck there, but if you can't say it you are in big trouble. You need to complain. You can't stuff the feelings. You need a support system. You need to say things you thought you couldn't imagine yourself saying. Call a friend. You've got be heard, and you've got to be open with your feelings. If you can't find a way to share those most awful feelings, you cannot go on.

We are all tempted to look at another person's situation with envy. We're jealous of those who seem to have more or to have it easier. But someone is always richer, luckier, or healthier. We can spend our lives being bitter, or we can look at our own lives with different eyes and see how blessed we are. What is really important? What really matters? I can look outside myself. I can have a larger view of life.

People often say to us, "We couldn't do what you do." The truth is, you do what you have to. There's that line we've all gotten so tired of hearing: "God never gives you anything you can't handle." I don't want to be in a position to know how much harder it could be. This feels like enough, thank you very much. We don't always get to choose what we get in life. And that's a big thing for me, recognizing what we can choose and what we can't choose. Being angry and bitter isn't useful for anybody. I can say to others that, no matter what, you can live through it and you will. And I live that myself, one day at a time. That's the one big lesson.

NORTON AND BEVERLY STILLMAN

*These days, we hear a lot about middle-aged children
taking care of aging parents. As life spans lengthen,
increasing numbers of "children" in their sixties, seventies,
and even eighties are taking care of elderly parents. This was
the situation for Norton and Beverly Stillman, a brother
and sister who, in their sixties, were living with and caring
for elderly parents. The day that their dad stumbled on the
steps, knocking over their mother as he fell and causing her
to break her hip, Norton and Beverly decided it would be
best for their parents to come and live with them. They told
me of their deep love, respect, and admiration for their
parents, who, Norton said, had left them "a legacy on how
to make the world a better place in which to live."*

*I was invited to come to Norton and Beverly's home to
talk with them about their caregiving experience. The
dining room table was covered with photos of their parents
and other mementos. It was obvious that this had been a
close, caring relationship. Norton began the conversation.*

The folks lived with us for almost five years. It was probably an advantage that neither of us is married. We didn't have the other family concerns and obligations that many people have, so we were able to devote full attention to taking care of our parents.

During those years when my sister and I were caregiving, we were together as a family all the time. Through good times and bad, we got very close. Our mother was very fragile in her last years. She could barely talk, she was so weak. But how she handled her diminished health taught us something important. She was a caring, gentle, and considerate person, always thanked people who were helping her, and was able to smile, right up to the end.

I used to travel a lot, but during those years when Mother and Dad lived with us I gave that up. I knew someday my role as a caregiver would end and I'd do my traveling then. Mother died when she was ninety. About ten days before she died, she told me how much she appreciated that we had taken care of her and thanked us for all we had done for her. It was amazing that she could summon up the energy to say that. It meant a lot.

During those years when my sister and I were caregiving, we were together as a family all the time. Through good times and bad, we got very close.

Dad always had an upbeat attitude. About three or four days before he passed away, I remember saying to him, "Hey, you seem to feel a little better today," and he smiled and said, "Why not?" He never made a big thing about small stuff. His attitude was always positive, and you could hear it in his favorite phrase, "Why not?"

Beverly came into the room at that point, talking of her father as she served tea.

Just thinking of him now as we talk warms my heart because he was so full of energy for life and laughter, and he enjoyed everything so much. Everyone in his presence felt this sense of joy as well. There was a warm conversation and an exchange, and I seemed always to be learning new things from him. He continued to teach me how to be a good person—how to be a religious and observe religious holidays with meaning. He taught us to enjoy life and make the most of life. Both Mother and Father were strong in their beliefs. Mother had her concerns about social equality, and Dad had his religious convictions and practices. They taught us by their example to stand up for what we believe.

In his later years, Dad did have some dementia, but we continued to have conversations and enjoy each other's company. I helped to keep my dad alert. I kept talking to him all the time, even when we were watching television. I'd say things like, "That man on TV has a red tie just like yours" or "Oh, look at that person's blue eyes." It would keep his mind active. He worked hard to remember things and keep thinking because he knew he had times of memory lapses and confusion. He never really lost touch. He knew both of us by name until the end. And we always took him places with us. We didn't want him to think of himself as being different and unable to function in a social situation. Sometimes he would drop things on the floor or make a mess at the table, but we weren't embarrassed. We were glad to have him with us. He always liked to feel important, so we kept our attention on him when we were with others. If he had been in a nursing home, he probably would have just been sitting there, but we kept him doing things as long as he could. At the end, he lost

Norton and I never regretted what we gave up to take care of our mother and father.
We had good times with them up until the end, and we were blessed because we had friends and family around.

his mobility and had difficulty standing up, so we had some help come into the house. Up until then we managed.

I know that Norton and I never regretted what we gave up to take care of our mother and father. We had good times with them up until the end, and we were blessed because we had friends and family around. There were always people in the house. Everything we did for our parents was with love. The legacy they left us is love.

PAM COSTAIN

Pam Costain is the Executive Director of the Resource Center of the Americas in Minneapolis, Minnesota. Her public life in itself could be all-consuming, yet her private life includes a husband and children and the responsibility of caring for her eighty-eight-year-old mother, who now lives in a nursing home not far from her. Recently, Pam wrote an editorial for the local newspaper, titled "It's a Gift to Participate with Mom in the Process of Aging." I called Pam and asked if I could come and talk with her. The first question I asked her was why she wrote the piece. There was passion in her voice when she told me that she believed she had gained some insights into the care of a loved one that would be useful to other people. Pam and I talked for quite a while about caring for her mother—an experience she describes as "a difficult blessing."

B eing a caregiver is such a profound and stunning experience for me that I needed to write about it. I'm pro-
cessing this at a higher level than I do my daily life
because everything is coming at me new. I didn't know anything about caring for a parent when I entered the world of
caregiving.

My mother lived alone in her own home in another city
and drove a car until about three years ago. When she began
to show signs of confusion, she went to live with my sister.
Now that I've taken on the responsibility of my mother's
care, I can reflect on what it was like for my sister to manage
her care for as long as she did. I can remember when we first
noticed that my mom was acting strangely. She lost the ability to cook. She'd try to make
her favorite dessert, and an
ingredient would be missing or
it would be burned. Or she'd
try to make cookies that she'd
made a hundred times before,
and she couldn't do it.

One of my biggest revelations about Alzheimer's, or dementia of any kind, is that there's no point in attempting to adjust somebody's reality.

Mother always had kept a
meticulous checkbook, but we went through her checkbook
and found she had completely lost control of paying bills and
writing checks. This signalled to us that something was really wrong. We could see we were dealing with some kind of
dementia. The doctor labeled it "Alzheimer's."

One of my biggest revelations about Alzheimer's, or
dementia of any kind, is that there's no point in attempting
to adjust somebody's reality. There is no point in arguing or
correcting my mother. I came to understand this intuitive-
ly. When I wrote the editorial for the newspaper, I made
this a main point because I've found that acceptance is easier for both me and her. I'll read you a paragraph from that
editorial:

When my mother and I talk and her mind is clear, I rejoice in the give-and-take, the chance to tease her and even to get her to smile. When her mind is fuzzy, I appreciate the opportunity to just be there—listening, getting her to smile, helping her to reenter the world and connect with me. When her mind is completely gone, I actually enjoy entering her fantasy world and going where it takes me.

My mother likes to talk about having just seen her mother, my grandmother, who's been dead for several decades. She's walking down the hallway, she's going back to her home town, she's brought my mother a stuffed animal—things like that. I've learned to let go. As long as her delusions aren't frightening or harmful to her, I just play with it, and we have a fanciful conversation within her reality. What does it matter if it isn't my reality? It works for me to enter into hers. I feel best

Sometimes I'll have my arm around her and she'll put her head on my shoulder, and we have a very sweet and close moment. She never would have done that when she was her old independent self.

when I just go with it. But sometimes she is very clear in her thinking, and my mother is back with me. For a short while, she has complete recall, and when that happens it's really fun. She never used to demonstrate affection, and now we often have tender moments when she'll let me hold her hand. Sometimes I'll have my arm around her and she'll put her head on my shoulder, and we have a very sweet and close moment. She never would have done that when she was her old independent self. That just wasn't her mode when she was more in control of her behavior.

Mom isn't very happy most of the time, but seeing familiar faces cheers her up. Our family has a lake cabin, and when we take her there and family and friends show up, it makes her very happy. My sister got married this past summer at the lake, and we made a big deal about the wedding, partly for my mom because it was a way to ask a lot of people to come see her and be with her. Frankly, from the day the wedding was announced, it was her entire focus. I know, too, when I go to visit her—which is at least three times a week—it makes her happy. She has wonderful care in the place she's in now, far better than the first nursing home we had her in, but she doesn't seem to respond much to her surroundings. She's very much aware of her losses—the loss of her independence, her home, her car, her control over her money. Yet, although she's aware of all these things, she can't really put together what has happened to her. She understands that everything has changed, but she doesn't have the ability to analyze it.

I was very frustrated with Mother's lack of care, and my tears were about the whole institutional approach— the bureaucracy and the fighting over medical systems and money.

My husband and my two children (ages nineteen and twenty-three) have been wonderfully supportive of me, really there for me in terms of giving me a place and space to process this. I have to come home and tell my family about my visit with Grandma. They might be bored, but they always let me talk. They've shared both my laughter and my tears. The tears come from real physical exhaustion. There was a time when my job was more difficult and demanding than it had ever been, and, between that and my mother, I got to a point where I cried for about a month. I just couldn't balance everything.

Another set of tears came when my mother was in a previous nursing home. I was beside myself with grief and anger, and I couldn't control anything that was happening. Many caregivers feel helpless to get the care they want for their parent. I was very frustrated with Mother's lack of care, and my tears were about the whole institutional approach—the bureaucracy and the fighting over medical systems and money. Poor food, lousy care, smelly hallways—fortunately, that's not where my mom is now, but that's where she could be. My tears and exhaustion were more about the fights to get adequate care for my mom than the deterioration of my mom's functioning. We're in a culture that has not yet thought this through. Our society, which already has so many older people that need nursing home care, has just not planned for what it's going to take to care for the frail and elderly in the future. I know these problems can't be solved easily, but shouldn't there be a way to make humane care more widely available?

Our society, which already has so many older people that need nursing home care, has just not planned for what it's going to take to care for the frail and elderly in the future. I know these problems can't be solved easily, but shouldn't there be a way to make humane care more widely available?

I'm conscious of wanting to model something for my kids. I hope my children will hang in there with me when I'm old and in need of care. I hope that helping me with my responsibilities for my mother will make a difference in how they view things. Before this, my kids knew their grandma the way other kids know their grandmas. They visited her a couple times a year, she baked them cookies, and they didn't particularly let her in their lives. They liked her fine because she was their grandma, but they didn't have a very deep emotional attachment. So now they have a chance to really know her.

One Saturday night, for example, I was out with my husband, and my younger daughter was home with a friend. They were about to go out to a party when Grandma called. She was clearly distressed and needed somebody. My daughter went right over there with her friend. In some ways, that seems like a very little thing, but in this culture for a teenager to give up her Saturday night when she was about to go party with friends and respond first to her grandma's needs—well, that's something, I think. It was an incredible night, because instead of spending ten minutes with Grandma, my daughter stayed over two hours. She ended up reading inspirational verse to her. The words probably meant very little to my daughter, but she figured out that this would be calming and meaningful to her grandmother. Even though it was only one experience, I think it was an important lesson for my daughter. When we discussed the evening, I could see she got a lot from it. It was a lesson in compassion and understanding—a real gift.

I don't want to romanticize this situation, but I've come to believe that becoming my mother's caregiver has been a real gift. I think about some of my friends whose mothers died without a prolonged physical or mental degeneration that required caregiving. On the one hand they missed the really difficult process of decline, which is horrific; but on the other hand they missed the opportunity for this very special relationship that I have had.

I'm learning something about living, something about being a human being, that I might never have learned if this hadn't happened. My sister couldn't do it anymore, and we had run out of options. It wasn't well thought out. My mother just landed in my town and in my life. I didn't choose it, but I now consider it a miracle that it happened. I didn't understand or appreciate then what the caregiving experience could give to me. I truly feel a gratitude that the circumstances were such that I almost didn't have any choice but to take her. I don't want to romanticize this situation, but I've come to believe that becoming my mother's caregiver has been a real gift. I think about some of my friends whose mothers died without a prolonged physical or mental degeneration that required caregiving. On the one hand they missed the really difficult process of decline, which is horrific; but on the other hand they missed the opportunity for this very special relationship that I have had.

As a caregiver, you really have to stay in the present. If you aren't in the present, it's really an awful task. You can't think of what you have to do outside of being there. It doesn't matter what should have been or could have been, because it just is what it is. When I'm with my mom, I have to let go of the world, enter the nursing home, and be there for her. None of the time orientation that runs our lives means anything to my mom. All she cares about is that I'm sitting there with her now. It's wonderful to realize that if you let yourself stop and just be there in the present for someone that really needs you—that's a lot for a human being to get in life. That's a tremendous gift, just to make someone really happy.

We don't often feel like we've made a difference in the world, and this is a very concrete thing. Often, when I'm busy with things in my life, I make myself visit Mom. I don't really want to, I've got a lot of other things I must do, and I'm really hard-pressed for time. So sometimes I go to visit her with a little bit of an edge, and then I spend a couple of hours with her, and I walk out and say to myself, "What was I obsessing about? This was a really nice thing to do, for both my mom and me. It's given me something back that's really nice." And I leave the nursing home smiling.

PEG KOLM

Peg and I knew each other in our "carefree years." We worked together at National Public Radio in Washington, D.C. We were both single and totally preoccupied with our exciting and stimulating jobs. We were somewhat oblivious to the problems and challenges one often faces as lives become more complicated. I look back on those days and think about how unaware we were of the challenges that might confront us in the future. Eventually, Peg married her boyfriend, Rich, had a son, and two years later was pregnant again. It wasn't very long ago that I had an opportunity to spend the day with Peg. It was our time to catch up on the years we'd been out of touch. Peg talked about the birth of her daughter, Kate, who was born with a rare genetic defect called <u>CHARGE</u> Syndrome. Kate is ten years old now. Peg's tale has no last chapter. It's an ongoing story.

When I was pregnant with Kate, I had no idea there was anything wrong. The birth of my son had been easy. I figured Kate's birth would be fine, too. I went into labor five and a half weeks early. At the hospital, I was losing blood, so the doctors did an emergency Caesarean section. It was a hard birth. I almost didn't make it. That was the day when life as we'd known it ended.

Most people don't know much about the genetic malady CHARGE that Kate was born with. Why bother going into it? It's such a long song and dance. When people ask what's wrong with Kate, I tell them that I'll explain it to them after they meet her or they'll expect to see a monster. I want to show them that she's a great kid.

When people ask what's wrong with Kate, I tell them that I'll explain it to them after they meet her or they'll expect to see a monster. I want to show them that she's a great kid.

CHARGE Syndrome is an acronym for the different parts of the body in which abnormalities appear: C stands for coloboma; H for heart defects; A for atresia of the choanae; R for retardation of growth and development; G for genital and urinary abnormalities; and E for ear abnormalities and/or hearing loss. They tell me that the genetic defect occurred about thirty-five days into the pregnancy. It's very rare, and hardly anything is known about it. Up until about fifteen years ago most of the babies with CHARGE Syndrome never survived birth.

Kate's ears are malformed and abnormal. She's been tested as moderately to severely deaf. Kate does have some hearing on one side, and if she would wear a hearing aid, which she won't, she could hear some. Her nasal passages are blocked with bone. She has a couple of minor heart problems. She's considered legally blind, but thankfully she does have some vision. She doesn't look at people's faces, but she doesn't walk into things—she manages. Her esophagus has been surgically repaired. She has a button, or a gastric tube, that allows her to be fed through her stomach. She can't drink liquids, so that's a problem. She needs to be pump-fed; she can't swallow well. She eats some food by mouth—actually only yogurt, blueberry yogurt. She's so opinionated and stubborn; she sure knows what she wants! She's a strong-willed child.

I'm thinking back on when I saw Kate for the first time in the ICU. My husband Rich was saying to the nurses, "You've got to tell the doctors to call her Kate, not baby. We gave her a name, make them use it." And I remember him fussing with her, handling a baby that is in really bad shape, playing with her, and saying, "It's okay, Katie," just like she was normal. He kept talking to her and touching her and giving her positive strokes. I know his heart was breaking. I think it was hurting him more than me. At that time, I couldn't get past my shock to even feel the hurt, yet Rich was reaching out and loving her. It was so beautiful. I was so moved.

Sometimes one of us will experience anger or disappointment, but we never keep our feelings from each other. I think it's good we aren't trying to protect each other or hide from our own feelings.

A lot of beautiful things have happened between my husband and me since Kate was born. Very early on, Rich and I made an unspoken pact that we wouldn't edit our feelings about Kate. Sometimes one of us will experience anger or disappointment, but we never keep our feelings from each other. I think it's good we aren't trying to protect each other or hide from our own feelings. This was, and is, important: a gift. It's one way we share this burden.

My husband and I had to eventually face what was true for us. We had to let go of trying to beat the predictions. It took a long time. These changes in how you think don't happen in an instant. We thought if we just tried harder, if we just asked more questions, if we just found out more.... For a time, we were consumed with thinking about what might be. Might she walk? Talk? And yet her critical clinical picture was often so severe that it overshadowed everything. The professionals wanted to keep trying with her, even though they didn't know for sure what her outcome would be. They didn't encourage us to institutionalize her, and, frankly, I don't know what institution would have taken her.

I did what I needed to do, but it wasn't easy. For the first year of her life, my mothering instincts seemed to go away. I knew how to be a mom to my son, Richard, but with Kate I couldn't figure it out. I felt like a failure. I just didn't know how to be Kate's mom yet. I was like her case manager. I'd get involved with all kinds of specialists, doctors, and nurses. They would come to the house and suggest I try this or that, but every time I looked at her I couldn't get past the shock.

The turning point for me was when Kate got sick. Three waves of doctors saw her every day; they'd look at her like this specimen. I wanted them to see her as a child.

The turning point for me was when Kate got sick at the age of one year. She kept getting sicker and sicker, so we took her into the hospital and she was there for over two weeks. It was a teaching hospital, and three waves of doctors saw her every day; they'd look at her like this specimen. I wanted them to see her as a child. I remember thinking that, even if she was a mess, she's so cute! I remember actually falling in love with her. I talked to the nurses about how great Kate was, and I'll bet they thought I was out of my mind. But I fell in love with her the way others had fallen in love with her before me. My mother just adored my child from the moment she was born. She picked out the beautiful stuff: her eyebrows, her fingers. She'd praise the good things. By the time we came home with Kate, I was finally her mom. "Okay, this is it," I thought. "We aren't going to beat this. I'm going to be her mother. Other people can educate her and do her speech therapy. I'll mother her."

Most parents with kids like this keep thinking they'll find some new discovery, some new doctors with new information, or some hopeful thing through a support group. But it gets old. No more fixing. I realized Kate would make small progress from time to time. My hopes and dreams for Kate to be normal had to go. I decided to look at what she gave me and be happy with whatever it was.

Kate is now ten years old. She's quite small. You might think she is only a couple of years old. She wears a size five dress. Kate doesn't talk, but she does communicate; she's quite clear about things. She's bright. I don't know what her IQ is, but I'd guess she's on the level of a two- or three-year-old. She knows where things she wants are in the house. If she wants something, like food, she will walk over, get me, and walk me to the refrigerator. She goes to a special school for mul-

My hopes and dreams for Kate to be normal had to go. I decided to look at what she gave me and be happy with whatever it was.

tiply disabled children from 9:00 to 3:00, five days a week. She's in a very active program. It's like a preschool with smaller goals, but real goals. She's busy, and there is a ratio of three kids to one adult, so it's great.

Kate is so stimulated at the school during the week that on the weekends she tends to get in trouble. She needs constant attention. When she's home, she needs structure constantly. It's hard. I just hired someone who will come and stay on Saturdays. That will give me a break. I need time away to do things, to take care of the other parts of my life.

Kate is lots of fun to be with. My husband has a set of amazing games with her. He's kept his sense of humor and plays with Kate and laughs with her. It makes her more human to us, and that's healing. It's his way of really loving her and making her kid-like, not patient-like. Our son, Richard, for a while, didn't notice Kate much. Later on, he became more aware of her. Then he'd ask when she was going to come to his school. I'd always say, "Well, she's taking her time," and I'd let him know she was slow. Now that Richard is twelve, he understands she won't ever catch up. He says some kids tease him about Kate. But the kids that come over to the house like her and actually play with her. Sometimes Richard scoops her up and sits her down with his friends. It's not perfect, but Kate is part of the family.

One day, I had a discussion with a child psychiatrist at the hospital. I went into this whole thing about my worries and what might be in the future, and he said, "Stop! All we are really given is just this moment. That's it." Sometimes you're ready to hear what is being said, and I heard it. That conversation taught me something in a very deep way. The anxiety and worry shifted. What you can learn from having a child that could die at any

What you can learn from having a child that could die at any minute is to live in the moment. It was a gift to me.

minute is to live in the moment. It was a gift to me. Let's not worry about anything but whether she wakes up. And when she wakes up, we'll be present and in that moment. The future isn't part of my thinking.

To this day, I still grieve the child I didn't have. I was very busy right after Kate was born, but when things were quiet I would have bouts of deep crying. I would see little kids that looked a little like Kate and sink. I remember a time when I took care of my niece for a day. I didn't think I could do it. I took her to the park, but by the end of the day I was sobbing. The contrast was too great.

Once I was in a panel discussion at Kate's school with other parents. The last question was, "If you could have had anything from our community of support, what would you want?" I'm thinking things like a trip to a sunny place like the Bahamas or a housekeeper for a year—all sorts of things like that. A woman beside me spoke up and said, "You're basically asking me if you can take this away? No, you can't buy your way out. River runs through. There is no way out." I looked at her and realized she was so right. You don't get to take this away.

But I want to have fun and have a normal life. We have parties, friends over. I want to be cheerful and happy. I have every reason to be depressed and angry, and I've been there. Thank God, it fell away. I choose not to go there now. I am much less volatile, less anxious, than I used to be. I've gotten over the feeling I had done something wrong to have this kid. I was healthy, I took good care. It just happened. It is not my fault.

I've gotten over the feeling I had done something wrong to have this kid. I was healthy, I took good care. It just happened. It is not my fault.

There are times now when, as the expression goes, I can actually "lighten up." I'm able to look back on situations in our household and smile, even laugh. Some circumstances are actually funny. When Kate was about five, my mother-in-law broke her hip and was confined to a wheelchair. She needed constant care and wasn't getting it at home, so we said we'd bring her into our home. She lived with us for about a year and a half with twelve-hour-a-day professional care. Halfway through she had trouble swallowing. She finally got her own stomach tube and was fed like Kate. I remember one evening sitting at the table having dinner with my husband and our son. It was a normal dinner hour just like anybody else might have, except that Kate was buzzing around the living room and my mother-in-law was in the back room with a TV blaring while mumbling loudly to her aide. And that was our nutty household!

What are my hopes? I hope my husband and I will stay married. I know some relationships fall apart over these things. And I certainly hope our son will grow up healthy and become a good adult. I don't want him to suffer because of Kate. That's about it.

My husband and I will be caregivers for the rest of our lives. Our lives are filtered through Kate's situation. It will be forever. We need to start thinking about when we are too old and can't do it anymore. But one thing we know for sure is that the most important thing for us is to have large wells of love for Kate and not let anything ever get in the way of that love we feel for her. She's the strangest mixture of bitter and sweet I've ever known and, for me, the dearest thing on earth.

RACHAEL STAUFFER

*When I met Rachael, she was the teenage kid of my
landlord, Richard, a brilliant architect. I had taken a job
far from my hometown and needed to lease a small
apartment. I moved into the third floor of a charming
building that housed Richard's office and the offices of two
other architects. We became friends, the kind of friends you
make an effort to hold onto when you move. It was
through Rachael that I heard about Richard's stroke, and
that her father would be temporarily moving in with her.
That's how we all ended up once again living in the same
city and that's how Rachael and her dad became a chapter
in this book.*

I don't really think of myself as a caregiver. When I think
of a caregiver, I think of someone who is more involved
with daily care. My dad isn't that infirm, he isn't
bedridden. He gets around. He makes some of his own meals,
brushes his teeth, and bathes himself. He can go to the store,

count change, things like that. It's not high maintenance like many caregiver stories you hear. But I guess I'm in this for the long haul, so in that sense you could call me a caregiver.

When my dad was fifty-eight, he had a stroke. That was about twelve years ago. It left him unable to speak or write. It was a real tragedy because he was a creative, successful architect. Now his only method of communication is drawing pictures and pantomiming. I'm his main link with the outside world. My communication with him is basically a game of twenty questions. As he gets tired, later in the evening, it gets more difficult for him to communicate, and the harder he tries, the harder it is for him to get the words out, so it can become frustrating. We live a couple blocks from each other, and not a day goes by without my stopping over to bring something, pay his bills, watch over his portfolio, or deal with other things related to his care. I've had to take on all this and learn about it. That learning curve for me was difficult; it required some rearranging of my life.

I got caught up in the minutia of things and lost track of the big picture.

My parents were living on the East coast when Dad had the stroke. My mom took charge of everything; I had already moved away from home. Then my mom died quite unexpectedly. That was five years ago, and that's when I came into the picture. Dad moved to the city where I live. My only sister had died quite young, so I was the only immediate family he had left. For a period of time, after my mother died, things got really difficult for me. It was just too much. I had to pack up their whole house and move everything into a place near me. Moving Dad to a strange city eliminated many of his activities and took away the few friends that he had. The move was very stressful for both of us.

I guess what happened then was that I got caught up in the minutia of things and lost track of the big picture. I had taken a three-month leave of absence from my work, and we were spending a lot of time playing cards together. Meanwhile, I hadn't done any interviews to find caretakers for when I went back to work, I hadn't gone out to check on different living situations for him, and I hadn't made any effort to replace some of the activities and services he had before he moved here. I sort of became a little girl and lost my confidence to go out in the world and make adult, responsible decisions. I was hiding behind games of gin rummy.

But, you know, my mother had just died, my dad had unexpectedly become my responsibility, and I was angry and depressed; now I realize my dad was, too. I think most of my anger was really aimed at my mother, who had abandoned both of us. I hadn't had any grieving time to work out the loss of my mom. I didn't know what to do with my feelings. I ended up feeling very guilty because I would dump on my dad, and that sure wasn't fair. I

Being able to ask for help, that's something I've now learned. That's my big learning out of this experience.

finally realized I needed therapy and medication. I needed support to face what I had to deal with, and I needed help to get my own life on track again.

Being able to ask for help, that's something I've now learned. That's my big learning out of this experience. I grew up believing that you couldn't rely on other people and that if you wanted something done, you had to do it yourself. I've learned you can't survive that way. We need other people—friends, contacts, professionals. I've learned to reach out to others. My mother never could do this. She was what they call a "24/7" caregiver, and she took care of Dad all the time, never asking anyone for help, never living her own life. Toward the end of her life, when she was dying of lung cancer, a friend of the family came over to visit. She noticed that my mom could barely get out of bed and told my dad that something wasn't right. As well as he could, my dad said to this lady, "Yes, yes, she's sick," but my mom just wouldn't give in and ask for help. I lived in another city, and my mom didn't tell me how things were with her. When she finally got medical help, we discovered that my mom's lung had collapsed. She died one week later. She had no medical care prior to that. I think Mom was stubborn and in denial because she didn't know what would happen to Dad if she wasn't there to care for him.

Like my mom, I didn't understand how to reach out to others—that I needed to rely on others and they'd be there for me. Now I've arranged for others to take Dad places when I'm at work—drive him to appointments, bring him to his stroke support group, go with him to the market or the speech therapy class, take him to his Tai Chi class, make possible all those things that make his life better.

I've learned a lot about myself through my dad's problems. I've really grown up. I never would have believed in my wildest dreams that I was actually capable of doing all this stuff. It's built a lot of self-confidence.

Some of my friends have asked why I didn't just have my dad move in with me, instead of going to all the trouble and expense of setting him up in his own place. Well, first of all, the independence is better for him. But the other thing is that I've had a pattern of merging too easily into my parents' lives, and these past five years or so I've been working hard to establish my own life and separate what my own needs and wants are, to really become my own person. I had to avoid a situation where I was just my dad's caregiver and daughter. If this had all happened ten years earlier, that's what would have happened; I would have dropped everything in my own life. But I've grown a lot since then. I look back and know that I probably would have quit my job, stayed at home, been the good daughter, always there at his side. That's what my mom did, and I would have just taken over her role.

I've come to grips with the fact that it's not within my ability to make Dad happy. I know he's somewhat depressed; he's had his share of losses. But I can only do what I can do, and I've accepted that reality. The other thing I've learned is that I have a lot of patience, and knowing that has certainly helped. My friends will witness Dad trying to communicate something to me and how long it takes, and it makes them nervous. I just sit down, and we slowly go back to square one. It's taken persistence and patience, and thankfully I've discovered I've got both. I've learned a lot about myself through my dad's problems. I've really grown up. I never would have believed in my wildest dreams that I was actually capable of doing all this stuff. It's built a lot of self-confidence.

My partner and I often discuss our retirement, and we talk about having a house with an attached apartment for Dad. He's part of our long-term picture and our future plans. Dad is seventy now and in almost perfect physical health. One day, I was joking with him and I said, "You know, in thirty years when you're one hundred and in a wheelchair, I'll probably be in one, too." For a moment we laughed at the idea of us both going down the street in wheelchairs; then we both started to cry because there's a likelihood that it could actually happen.

RICHARD AVEDON

I first met Richard Avedon in July 1970. Avedon was at the Minneapolis Institute of Arts getting ready for what was labeled "the first showing of his serious work." I was a middle-aged returning student in graduate school at the University of Minnesota, working part-time at the campus radio station as an arts reporter. I remember arriving at the museum as Avedon was preparing to take a break from hanging the exhibition. A dozen reporters had waited patiently for an interview but were eventually told there would be no possibility for questions. Most of the reporters left. Being persistent and determined, I followed Richard Avedon into the park across from the museum. I approached him with a request for a brief conversation, and, when he surprised me by saying yes, I turned on my tape recorder, and we began discussing the obvious subject, his photography. Unexpectedly, our conversation took a turn, and I found myself listening to the poignant and personal story of Avedon's relationship with his father.

Over the last years of his father's life, Avedon took an
extensive series of photos of him. The portraits chronicle the
elder Avedon as he changed from an alert, well-dressed
man in his eighties into a withered victim of terminal can-
cer. To the question often put to him about this series of
photographs—"What kind of a son would take pictures of
his dying father?"—Avedon responds that the photos do not
represent only his father, or what he felt for his father, but
anyone at the end of life.

Some of the conversation that you'll read here was
originally heard as a public radio broadcast in 1970.
Several years later, I had another opportunity to interview
Richard Avedon when an exhibition of his photographs was
on view in Washington, D.C. Some of that conversation is
included here as well.

We weren't very close as father and son, actually not
close at all. When I was young, he was a school-
teacher and had a very tough life. I think he felt
that he could give me the kind of education that would
strengthen me for a world that he saw as a battle. But the
nature of his intelligence simply wasn't the nature of mine; I
was born with a visual intelligence. The pressures to learn
from him, his way, were too strong, and there was never a
sense of coming to the end of what his demands were. If I
would only concentrate! Whatever he was good at, I was not;
whatever he was interested in, I wasn't. And what I was interested in, he had no way of understanding. I slipped to another life, and that other place lasted my entire life as far as my
father was concerned. We had very little to say to one another. When he was in his sixties, his marriage to my mother
broke up, and he moved to Florida. Over the years, as my son
grew up, I had this vivid realization that there was this
stranger, living in Florida, who was my father and my son's
grandfather.

It was a very conscious effort that brought me to Sarasota, Florida—a conscious effort to find my father. It had nothing to do with photography. It was to know him and to feel that there could be something between us. I have a strong sense, as life isn't meaningless, that we have to make whatever small meaning is possible out of the time we're here. I felt that if I never learned to love my father, I was betraying a possibility in life and an opportunity to pass something on to my own son. I have a great sense of continuity.

My father was retired. Now in his late seventies, he complained about everything, particularly about real estate values. At one point, I had one of those great strokes of insight that come to you every once in a while. I said, "Listen, Dad. You sit here on the porch talking about real estate values. You know about these things. I have some money. Why don't we go into business together?" It was perfect. For the first time in our lives we met. And I, now in my forties, was interested in what he knew. So there were phone calls in the middle of the night—"marinas are hot"—everything in him came alive. The conversations were fascinating. And I really did learn a great deal from him. We finally had something to talk about.

I smuggled him out of the hospital. I told him, "You don't have to die in the hospital. We can go out and have a good time."

At a certain point in the euphoria, I realized that it's always the same story: He's the father, I'm the son, he knows nothing about me. In my need to know him better, I was hyping up an interest in real estate that I really didn't have. It will never work unless it's equal. I wrote to him—and it's the only letter of mine he ever kept. The letter said: "I've learned your business, now I'm going to ask you to learn mine. Photography means to me what real estate means to you, and I hate giving the best that's in me to strangers and nothing to you."

The next time I came down to Florida, I brought an eight-by-ten camera, an assistant, a writer, and a tape recorder so he'd know I was serious. And every time I visited we had a photographic sitting. He learned what I wanted, and he was involved to the degree that he wanted to give me what I wanted. Finally we did speak each other's language.

> He has asked several times to see the pictures. I don't want to show them to him ... because I don't think he'll like them. Whenever he poses for me, he smiles and becomes benign, gentle ... and somehow wise. He would be very happy to see that picture of himself.
>
> My photographs show his impatience. I love that quality in him. But seeing it would frighten him. He isn't interested in the fact that he looks his age, eighty-three, and is still fantastically vibrant and angry and hungry and alive. He's much more interested in looking sage. So my sense of what's beautiful is very different from his.
>
> *—from Avedon's writings in the introduction*
> *to the catalog of his 1970 exhibition*
> *at the Minneapolis Institute of Arts*

Eight months before he died, my father had a major liver operation that he had absolutely no expectation of surviving. I wheeled him into the operating room, and he had a little sedation. This man, who had never heard of Beckett, who didn't know what the word *existential* meant, looked up at me and said, "Dick, is, is, isn't isn't." These might have been his last words if he had died. He expected he wouldn't live through the operation, but he lived for eight months.

Later, when he was on chemotherapy, I flew to Sarasota. We had a really good week together. I smuggled him out of the hospital. I told him, "You don't have to die in the hospital. We can go out and have a good time." He began to get an idea of what my sense of humor was like. We went all over. I showed him my life. I took him to Miami, and we did one more sitting. Then I went back to New York. The day I left, he stopped eating, and five days later he was dead. I believe he stayed alive to have those last photographs taken.

Now understand this: my work is not journalism and those pictures are not about the death of a man. Others have described them that way, but many of them were done when he was in perfect health. They're about a certain kind of man in the world, about his life and who he was. And then, too, those photographs are really about what it means to be any one of us at the end of our lives.

ROSALYNN CARTER

*In 1999 I produced an hour-long public radio program
entitled "Hardship into Hope: The Rewards of
Caregiving." As a matter of fact, this very book grew out of
the positive response to the broadcast. (The program has
been made available to you on the CD in the jacket inside
the back cover of this book.) One of the voices you'll hear
when you listen to the recording is that of former First
Lady Rosalynn Carter, wife of former President Jimmy
Carter. I was fortunate to be able to arrange a conversation
with Mrs. Carter, who wrote about the concerns of family
caregivers in her book,* Helping Yourself Help Others, *
published in 1994. Here are some of Rosalynn Carter's
comments that I recorded at our meeting.*

An enormous number of us at some time in our lives
will take on the responsibility of caring for another
person who is ill or incapacitated; or, possibly, we
ourselves will be the one in need of care. Caregiving has

certainly touched my life and my family. My father died when I was thirteen. I was the oldest of four children. My mother depended heavily on me to help her. Her mother, my grandmother, died the next year, and my grandfather came to live with us. He was seventy at the time, and he lived to be ninety-five. My mother also needed care in her later years. I was traveling so much that I couldn't give her the full-time care she required. When she was ninety-two, we made the very difficult decision to move her into an assisted living facility—a decision that was painful for us (as it is for many families), but she couldn't stay by herself any longer.

There are only four kinds of people in this world: those who have been caregivers, those who currently are caregivers, those who will be caregivers, and those who will need caregivers. That pretty much covers all of us.

My daughter-in-law was thrust into the role of family caregiver when her father died. Her mother, who lived five hours away, was miserable living by herself. She was equally miserable when she came to visit her daughter. It was a very serious and stressful situation. At the time, they had three little boys, and my daughter-in-law had to take care of her mother as well as the children, a common situation in many families. So I've experienced a whole range of caregiving in my family. I've also worked a good deal with people who were caring for the mentally ill. Ever since my husband was governor of Georgia in the early 1970s, the whole issue of caregivers has been very important to me.

When we came to Atlanta from the White House, our local college had a small endowment for mental health programs. We began working with persons who cared for the mentally ill. Our first big session was focused on caregiver burn-out. It also was open to people who were caring for those who were physically handicapped, frail, or elderly. This modest program started us working with caregivers in our community. When we established the Rosalynn Carter Institute, no group we knew of was working on the issue of caregiving. I called over thirty organizations, and not one had a program on caregiving. These days, people are beginning to realize that family caregivers need support systems for themselves as well for those they care for.

People might be surprised to learn that family members or friends attend to most persons needing care at home. Only 10 to 20 percent of those requiring care receive it from professional caregivers. Employers are recognizing the need to create support programs for their employees who, more and more, are regularly checking on loved ones at home, taking them to appointments, and attending to their many needs. These caregivers need support systems at the workplace as they juggle home and work responsibilities.

Family members or friends attend to most persons needing care at home. Only 10 to 20 percent of those requiring care receive it from professional caregivers.

When we first began our program, we interviewed hundreds of family caregivers. Almost every caregiver we talked with felt guilty if they weren't always with their loved one or on call every minute of every day. Many felt overwhelmed, isolated, burdened. But if a person can develop the attitude that caregiving is a volunteer job they've take on, something they've entered into willingly to help a loved one, then they feel freer to get outside help. A change of attitude, a shift in perspective isn't easy, but it makes all the difference.

Caregiving is very difficult. I always say that if you don't take care of yourself, then the quality of care you give to your loved one is diminished. The message that I would like to give to all caregivers, no matter what their personal situation, is that they must find some space in the day just for themselves. Make time, make space, have something outside of your caregiving that's your own. Get out if you can. Some caregivers can't, but they can have hobbies or other activities that relax and distract them and give them pleasure. One woman, who was responsible for caring full-time for her mother and tending her mother's large garden as well, recently told me she started taking photographs of the flowers. She ended up setting up a business selling her photographs!

When we did our survey, even the people whom we felt were the most burdened would tell us that they found much satisfaction and many rewards in caregiving. I remember talking with one woman who said, "I just wanted to run away from it all, and one day I did. I checked into a motel, left my father all alone in a wheelchair, stayed there a couple of hours before I felt so guilty that I went home." And then she said, "I can take better care, more loving care, of my father than anybody!" She felt real pride that she could do that, that she could do something to make someone else's life better.

The message that I would like to give to all caregivers, no matter what their personal situation, is that they must find some space in the day just for themselves.

It's important and extremely satisfying to keep communications open with the ones you're caring for. Let them share their feelings and fears with you as well. You can say something like, "I know how you must feel about this happening to your body. You must be sad; you must be angry." Acknowledging their feelings and fears makes communication so much easier. They can see then that you have compassion and empathy for them.

Physical touch is also really important. People who are ill feel helpless, damaged, that they're a burden. They no longer feel physically attractive or that they're lovable. For someone to touch them—put a hand on their brow or hold their hand—can make them feel that somebody really cares for them no matter how they look or feel, or what is wrong with them. You must let yourself feel the sadness, the frustration, the pain, and the anger of your loved one. And you must grieve your loved one's losses as well as your own.

If the media told good stories of family caregivers coping with their many challenges—stories about the trauma and stress of having to put a loved one in a home or other facility, and the sadness one experiences in giving up their own home—it would let caregivers know that they're not alone, that these things touch everyone. Caregivers often feel that they're isolated, that nobody cares about them, that what they're doing is thankless. It's important to let people know that caregiving for somebody is a very important thing, a very meaningful thing for a person to be able to do.

Profound learning often comes with caregiving. Hearing stories of caregivers helps prepare us all to be caregivers someday. Every household is going to face this issue at one time or another in some way. Like I've said before, there are only four kinds of people in this world: those who have been caregivers, those who currently are caregivers, those who will be caregivers, and those who will need caregivers. That pretty much covers all of us.

SHARON BUFFINGTON

Sharon Buffington is fifty-eight years old. She lives alone in a spacious, charming old home, surrounded by antique furniture and mementos of a life with her partner, Sheila, who passed away three years earlier. We sat comfortably in her fragrant and colorful backyard garden, sipping our iced tea as Sharon told me about Sheila and their life together.

Before we met, Sheila had been married and had four children. I've known her children for many years now, and they consider me like a second mom. When Sheila's father died and she was helping her mother clean out his closet, her mother said to Sheila, "You know, for over fifty years I was married to your dad, and I never really felt like I was loved." And Sheila thought, "I've just put in nineteen years unloved. I'm not doing anymore!" She subsequently got a divorce.

I met Sheila when I was thirty-nine; she was seven years older than me. We'd be together almost seventeen years. After

Sheila and I moved in together, one of our friends said that seeing the two of us leave for work gave her quite a laugh. Two lawyers, going to work—Sheila with her little Peter Pan collar, pearls, and her proper business suit. And then me in my hippie sandals, peasant skirt, and cloth briefcase.

Sheila had been a stay-at-home mom, but she was exceptionally smart. While in her forties, she took the required tests, got into law school, and eventually became the county law librarian. All the judges, lawyers, and law clerks loved her. When you were in a conversation with her, you knew she was really interested in you, and she was always doing things for everyone she knew. Sheila was a very special, unique person. She loved people, and when you were in her presence you always felt really special—everybody did.

When Sheila started getting sick, the only symptom she had was an uncharacteristic depression. Then she started doing odd things. Like one day a friend slammed her car door

We decided we didn't want to be away from each other, so I closed my law office, said good-bye to my secretary and my paralegal, and stayed at home to be with Sheila for the time we had left together.

shut while Sheila's finger was in the door. She never said a word, just pulled it out. She didn't cry out or say anything, but her finger was broken. Then she started having dizzy spells and fell a couple of times at work. The care the doctors suggested didn't help. She got worse every day. We finally went to the Mayo Clinic, and they found brain tumors. They did brain surgery and discovered that she had central nervous system lymphoma. It's very rare. Only about 2 percent of the population ever get this form of cancer. We had some big decisions to make. We decided we didn't want to be away from each other, so I closed my law office, said good-bye to my secretary and my paralegal, and stayed at home to be with Sheila for the time we had left together.

"I think I have this illness for a reason," Sheila told me. When I asked her to elaborate, she explained that she felt that having this disease was to teach people something important, to teach people about living and cancer. She asked that we make a conscious decision to deal with her illness with a positive perspective. So we made a pact that we weren't going to get angry about little stuff because we didn't want to use our energy that way. We immediately saw so many things in our lives that were small compared to what we were faced with now.

During the months that followed, I learned a lot about grace. I watched Sheila deal with things in an amazing way, things that for me would have been insurmountable. She had full brain radiation as well as chemotherapy. After the treatments, she would always thank the nurses. She was never cross or irritable. She never complained, not once. I never heard her say, "Why is this happening to me?" or "Why do I have to go through this?" As I watched her, I learned something very important about how to look at what comes to us during our lives. I began to see that questioning what you've been given isn't of any value because it keeps you stuck in the same place and actually looking backward. Through Sheila's example, I learned that when you're given something, that's what it is. The challenge is to find the best and most beneficial meaning out of that experience.

Through Sheila's example, I learned that when you're given something, that's what it is. The challenge is to find the best and most beneficial meaning out of that experience.

Over time, Sheila became more and more childlike. Somehow I was able to learn to accept and balance both the adult and the child in her. I couldn't have the same kind of conversations with her as I'd had in the past, but I realized that we just had to let our relationship shift. I took Sheila out for lunch every day so she would have some life out in the world, and I learned to put her needs, her moods, before mine. I'm sure it was the tumor that caused her to say inappropriate, crazy things out of context. Like one day when we were on an escalator and she yelled out, "Don't push me off!" Or we'd be at a friend's home talking and having tea, and she'd say, "Don't run over me with the car, Sherry." My challenge was to learn to live with things like this and not take what she blurted out that seriously.

Sheila lived five and a half years after she was diagnosed, but she was quite compromised after the surgery. It was important for me to spend all the time I could in those remaining years with Sheila. We developed a new kind of intimacy, a different kind of closeness because she became so childlike. I felt it was inappropriate to have an adult kind of physical intimacy with her, but we hugged and sat close and held hands. It was hard for me

Many of us struggle with feelings that we should always do more and more. You do what you can and accept that.

to leave her side even to take care of the dog, go shopping, or do the laundry. She always wanted me to be in the same room with her. One day, when I was out of the room for just minutes, she called out rather desperately, "Sherry, come in here now and be with me. I'm so lonesome!" During the last months of her life, I moved my computer right next to her bed so I could be there all the time.

I remember several things Sheila said to me toward the end. One day, out of nowhere she said, "You know, Sherry, it's always easier to be kind." I now try always to be considerate and understanding. I so often think how Sheila might react in a situation, and her words "Be kind" echo in my head. I've become more compassionate and sensitive to the mood and frame of mind of others.

I've learned other things as well from my caregiving experience. Martyring ourselves because we have to take care of another person doesn't help the situation at all. I want to caution people who are caring for a loved one to watch out for that. I used to ask myself, "Am I doing enough? Is there more I should do to make Sheila happy and comfortable? Am I spending enough time with her?" I know now that it accomplishes nothing to agonize about such things. And I know that many of us struggle with feelings that we should always do more and more. You do what you can and accept that.

Another thing: I was wrong not to let others help me. So many of our friends offered, but I'd say no. I was determined to do it all myself. They finally stopped asking and would just show up with a meal or ice cream, or insist on staying with Sheila while I went out. For some of us, it's hard to accept help. Yet, a person can't show that they're truly your friend unless you let them in and allow them to help. They want to be part of the caregiving process, and you deprive them of that if you don't allow them to participate.

I wouldn't trade those years I took care of Sheila for anything. I never made the house like a sick place. I always had colorful sheets on Sheila's hospital bed, flowers in the room, and tea and cookies when friends stopped over. For me, caring for Sheila was a joyful, marvelous thing. I never saw it as a hardship or a burden; I felt it was a wonderful journey and that I was privileged to be a part of it. I felt like I was giving back in some way the many years of giving and companionship that Sheila had given to me.

SHILA HAZAN

If I had met Shila and Morrie five years earlier, I would have thought that this attractive, smartly dressed couple had it all: a glamorous lifestyle, ease of travel to exotic destinations, everything that money can offer. But material wealth is no guarantee against the ravages of illness, dementia, and loss. Shila and Morrie are both past their midlife years now. Morrie has Alzheimer's, and Shila has the responsibility of his care. When she shared her story with me, it was a powerful reminder that privilege doesn't protect one from pain. "I know I'm blessed with the ability to pay for around-the-clock care for my husband, yet I also know that money doesn't solve all the problems one is faced with when illness changes everything in your life." Through Morrie's illness, Shila has found a wisdom that money just can't buy.

Morrie is my fourth husband. Finally I got it right! Before his illness, we traveled, we talked, we loved each other dearly. It was a life fully realized. He is, and always will be, the love of my life.

I really don't remember when the symptoms began. I guess it was about five and a half years ago. When I first consulted the doctors, they said, "No problem, just some little mini-strokes. We can take care of that with medication, and he won't have any more." But no medication seemed to help, and there was continuing deterioration.

In August of that year, we went on what turned out to be our last vacation. We flew to Alaska to take a cruise ship for what we had hoped would be a wonderful two-week trip. But it didn't turn out that way. The whole time Morrie was confused, had trouble understanding directions, and behaved unpredictably. I was so frightened that I couldn't let myself see what was happening. My denial was total. But then Morrie became unpredictably violent. There was no denying then that something was terribly wrong.

Morrie was confused, had trouble understanding directions, and behaved unpredictably. I was so frightened that I couldn't let myself see what was happening. My denial was total.

He started having trouble with numbers, and that was extremely disturbing to him. Morrie has always been involved in high finance, big business. His life was crunching numbers. Suddenly it seemed all he would talk about was money. The reality is that we are very well off financially, and there was no basis for his concern. Maybe he was remembering that he was born to poor Greek immigrants—a flower peddler who roasted nuts to supplement the family income—and Morrie's dream was to have a fruit stand of his own. Morrie got his fruit stand. It was the beginning of what eventually became an empire. Morrie became an entrepreneurial giant and amassed a fortune.

Now it's that wealth that supports his full-time, around-the-clock care. Of course, I'm aware that, with the kind of totally incapacitating illness my husband has, the money has been an enormous advantage. Financial security has assured the kind of paid professional caregiving help that makes an enormous difference. I'm blessed that I don't have the financial stress and worries that so many people do, but privilege doesn't take away the pain.

Morrie is severely demented now. We call it Alzheimer's, but that's just a label for a wide range of such situations. I've engaged warm, caring, competent people who take wonderful care of my husband. The violence that Morrie displayed at the onset isn't there anymore. The best medical advice we had was to simply stay out of verbal conflict with him; always assure him he's right and that we'll do things his way. His short-term memory is so bad he doesn't remember what he said anyway. We keep him calm and happy, and, whatever is going on in his brain, he thinks he's in control and doesn't feel threatened. Morrie doesn't respond well to care from a man, so now the entire staff I employ is female. I think he sees a man as a challenge, and he puts up a fight. The nurses call him "Papa Morrie," and they can get this big strapping man to do whatever they ask. I call the staff "Morrie's angels."

I'm blessed that I don't have the financial stress and worries that so many people do, but privilege doesn't take away the pain.

During the first two years of Morrie's decline I was physically ill, emotionally distraught, sleep-deprived, hysterical, and on the edge of a nervous breakdown. I tried medications, chiropractic, homeopathy, and acupuncture. All the things I tried at the physical level only gave me temporary relief. Psychotherapy and meditation were the two things that eventually enabled me to look for connections in the outside world that offered me comfort, peace of mind, and purpose.

That's when, through an acquaintance, I was introduced to the Science of Mind Church. It now has become my spiritual community. Although my cultural identification is with the Jewish religion, it was through the friendship with and support of the people at that church that I was able to reach the acceptance of what is, rather than being stuck in what could have been. I've learned that it's not what life deals you, but what you do with the hand you've been dealt. I've received an abundance of loving guidance and new learning. I've turned my potential "victim-hood" into what I've labeled "victor-hood." I've come to understand that today is all we have; this moment is what we have now.

My church has given me a way to reach out and help many people in need. I've found great comfort and satisfaction in giving money anonymously to help children and single mothers. I remember when I was raising two children alone, and many people did nice things for me without ever asking for anything in return.

I've found a way to consider Morrie's illness as a gift, an opportunity to grow and expand, to genuinely share and to help myself by helping others.

Now it's my turn to give. I give of myself and I give of my abundance. Thankfully I've discovered that being able to give is the most selfish pleasure in the world.

I know that I've made a difference by helping others. I've found a way to consider Morrie's illness as a gift, an opportunity to grow and expand, to genuinely share and to help myself by helping others. Today my goals are to experience deeper spiritual growth and involve my time and energy in outward service. I'm creating a rich and full life for myself. Certainly I have my sadness, but comfort comes from the quality of the life I'm leading and the people I've surrounded myself with. I feel encircled by a special energy from those around me. In spite of the tragedy of Morrie's illness, I truly believe my life is one of grace and blessing.

There have been many unexpected healings for me that have come out of Morrie's illness. At one time, I resented that Morrie's daughters didn't come to see him very often. I knew they felt mistrustful and frightened of me, and I of them. I had spent a lot of time being angry and resentful. That's all in the past. I've learned a lot about forgiveness. My negative feelings have been transformed into love and compassion. And that's the gift I've gotten out of this sad situation.

One daughter who lives out of town comes to visit now at least once a month, sometimes more if her husband has business in town. The other one who lives here doesn't come that often. A few years ago, I would have sat here with vitriol pouring out of me in resentment. Now I see what a hard time she must have seeing her father like this, and I have to respect her decisions on what she feels she can handle. I've forgiven myself for making judgments, and that has allowed me to forgive them. Morrie's son who lives out of town has told me he just can't come very often. It's too hard for him to see his father this way. I respect and accept his decision as well. He's been very kind and supportive. So I'm doing my best to get along in this world, and I believe they're doing the same. I'd say this change in my perspective is the greatest gift I've had out of all this.

There have been many unexpected healings for me that have come out of Morrie's illness. I've learned a lot about forgiveness. My negative feelings have been transformed into love and compassion.

Morrie is seventeen years older than I am so barring something unforeseen, he will probably die before me. It's interesting that I've already been through what I call the "widow syndrome," where everybody comes around for a few

weeks or months and then they disappear. I've already had
the people fall away who weren't going to be with me for the
long haul. If—I mean, when—Morrie dies, I will grieve
deeply. I know I'll be bereft for a time. But I won't have to
ask myself, "What will I do with the rest of my life?" I'm living the rest of my life right now. Mostly I live in a state of
gratitude for the ability to maintain him with every advantage. It's ironic, but as Morrie diminishes and his path
becomes more and more limited, I'm expanding and growing
on my path.

My relationship with my husband is no longer anything
like it was. I'm interchangeable with the nurses who take care
of him. I haven't been able to lie down next to him for a long
time. It's extremely painful for me. Only rarely do I cry now,
but when I do, the tears pour out. But then it's over. Maybe
it's sadness for what could have been or for who Morrie used
to be, yet I know there's no benefit in pursuing that kind of
thinking. Of course, it's distressing each time I see Morrie hit
a new low, but I guess I've learned to adjust to those changes;
the immediate feelings of fear and panic now pass quickly. I
consciously choose not to look ahead and anticipate what
will happen next.

Morrie and I are soul mates; I believe that and I remember that. Although he isn't the person I used to know, my
husband is still alive. I get to go in and kiss him, see that
wonderful smile and the twinkle in his eye, and feel his
warmth. I know that I'm truly, truly blessed.

VIVIAN GREENBERG

*Vivian is a social worker in private practice. She travels
across the country, conducting workshops and lectures on
the stresses of caregiving and relationship problems between
middle-aged adults and their aging parents. She didn't
consider herself a writer, but after caring for each of her
parents when they became ill and frail, she felt that she
had important things to say. In the book she subsequently
authored, she speaks of the time when we notice the signs of
frailty in our parents and we realize that they will grow
old and die. Vivian and I shared stories about our parents'
decline putting to end whatever fantasies of their
immortality we might have had. She told me, "I'm aware I
had some irrational feeling that as long as my parents were
alive I was protected from death. Being called upon to care
for them in their declining years taught me about life and
death and my limitations and my choices. I learned, and
not easily, the things that make the difference between caregiving as a stress and caregiving as a joy." I found Vivian to*

be a warm, compassionate, and generous conversationalist—a person who had gained maturity and developed wisdom from her caregiving experience.

I remember thinking that maybe I could write a book. I recall asking myself, "What do I know best of all?" And the answer was caregiving. I had much to say to those who are or have been caregivers for a parent. I know the hardships of caregiving—the anger, the resentment—yet I also know the rewards. I decided to use my clinical experience, as well as my personal experience, to write *Respecting Your Limits When Caring for Aging Parents.* I knew it couldn't be just intellectual, or it wouldn't truly reach the reader. It had to come from my heart.

I think that it's when our parents get old that we begin to recognize our own mortality.

My mother was a great cook, and she loved to prepare lovely lunches for me. Although I was an adult in my middle years when I came to visit my mother, I'd again become the little girl feasting on all her delights! One day, I came in and the table wasn't set. Mom said, "I haven't been able to set the table, will you help me? And maybe you could make the tuna salad. And would you wash the lettuce?" And from that day on, I realized that things would never be the same and that I couldn't pretend, even when mom invited me to lunch, that I was a little girl anymore. I think that it's when our parents get old that we begin to recognize our own mortality.

When my mother was diagnosed with Parkinson's disease, it was the beginning of my becoming a "primary caregiver." In the lexicon of gerontology, I was what is called a "distant caregiver," as I lived about thirty-five miles away. For quite a while, my father was wonderful in helping Mom with her care. My mother and I had a our own areas of interaction, partly because it was easier for her to tell me personal things about toileting and other functions related to personal care that she felt very private about.

Like most mothers and daughters, though, my mother and I had our difficulties. My mother was a very reserved person, and I tended to be somewhat wild in comparison. There were times when I really don't think she liked me very much. She would always compare me to soft-spoken girls. And I was never quite good enough for my mother. I played the piano, but my mother would tell me that my cousin played the piano better. I did well in school, but I didn't measure up in her eyes because another cousin was Phi Beta Kappa. There was always that friction there.

But when I became her caregiver, something wonderful happened. She thanked me many times for taking care of her. About ten or eleven years before she died, I went back to school to get a degree in social work, and my mother was so proud of me. She told me how wonderful it was that I was

> *Like most mothers and daughters, my mother and I had our difficulties. But when I became her caregiver, something wonderful happened.*

going to earn my own living, to be independent. And before she died she said to me, "I could never be jealous of anyone else's daughter." It seemed so easy for her to say these things. Suddenly I was something wonderful. I had triumphed in some way.

I'm a social worker. During the time I was taking care of my mother, I was on the geriatric evaluation team of a family medicine residency program. It was a situation where my personal life and my professional life converged. I ran a caregiver support group, and I used to see adult children who weren't taking care of their parents as I thought they should. They would tell of their parents making what they considered unreasonable demands. They didn't want to change their lives to give what they considered an excessive amount of time to their parents. Yet, here I was, running myself ragged going back and forth to attend to my mother. I remember thinking that I was better than they were, a more attentive and devoted child. I'm embarrassed to say that I was pretty judgmental in those days. Well, all that changed. I began to see that I was losing all sense of boundaries. I forgot that I had a self. Everything I thought or did was about her and what I could do for her, where I could take her, how I could fulfill her every need. I didn't count; I didn't matter. I was a "superwoman." I could do everything.

Eventually I came to realize how much time I was devoting to doing things for my mother, how obsessed I had become about serving her needs, and how it was taking big bites out of my life. I didn't have time or energy to do my job well, relax, read a book, play tennis, exercise, or even look at the newspaper. It was very unhealthy for me. I short-changed my husband as well. Some of us try and try, and when we don't succeed in serving all of our parents' needs, we feel more and more guilty; and then we get angry and feel terrible that we're angry, and the cycle starts all over again. I realize that I got into that trap with the care of my mother.

I had to fight that urge to always be there for her for everything. Unlearning that compulsion was my biggest challenge, my most important learning in being a caregiver.

I had to fight that urge to always be there for her for everything. Not that my mother expected it of me, but I expected it of me. I guess it was my image of what "good daughters" of that generation did. I recall a day when I had promised my mom I'd take off work and spend the day with her. I remember having a terrible migraine headache, yet I still went over to care for her. My feeling was that I was obligated to serve her no matter what. Unlearning that compulsion was my biggest challenge, my most important learning in being a caregiver. I hadn't set limits. I'm sure I'm not the only caregiver who has fallen into that pattern. One of the lessons I eventually learned was to understand that I'm not here just to take care of my parents and that I have a life that needs attention, too.

Once we went to a department store, and when my mother was trying on things, I wanted to help her. Because of her Parkinson's, she couldn't button or unbutton things fast or well, and my hands were always reaching out to do the buttons, the zippers, everything. My mother chastised me. "Vivian, leave me alone!" she said loudly. "There aren't many things left that I can do by myself, but I can do my buttons. If I fumble and I'm slow, you're just going to have to be patient."

I really learned something that day, and from then on I changed the way I operated. I learned to allow for her pace, and I learned to be comfortable and patient. I left plenty of time; I didn't want to be rushed. Actually, I wanted to savor every

One of the lessons I eventually learned was to understand that I'm not here just to take care of my parents and that I have a life that needs attention, too.

minute of being with her. She was tottering and frail, and I wanted to hold her arm and be with her and let her know that I was there for her on her terms. It became my special time with her, and there was great joy in that. I was grateful and still am for that insight that helped me develop patience.

The insights I gained during my caregiving experience were simple, yet profound. Our visits became really special; time almost stood still. We talked about many things. My mother loved to reminisce. She came to this country in 1923 and worked in the sweatshops of lower Manhattan. She had all kinds of stories to tell. She loved to talk, and I loved to listen. I really got to know my mother better and in a different way.

One of the big lessons I learned from caregiving is that I'm human: I have limits and I can only do so much. I had to learn to say no when I was her caregiver. Always saying yes or "of course I'll do that" takes a toll on the caregiver. I never totally integrated this learning when I was a caregiver for my mom. However, my father outlived my mother, and during the last four years of his life, I learned to say no and respect my limits. My dad would call me and ask me to leave work and take him to the bank. But instead of jumping in the car, I learned to say, "Dad, I have too much to do today. How about tomorrow?" And there would be a long pause, and he'd say, "Well, I guess that will be okay." He learned to see that I was busy, that I worked, that I had a family, that I had other commitments. I made a lot time for my father, but it worked best if we negotiated it. He knew I wasn't abandoning him; he was able to see my position. And I knew that if I paid attention to my needs I'd be a better caregiver.

One of the big lessons I learned from caregiving is that I'm human: I have limits and I can only do so much.

My father lived quite independently for four years after my mother died. Then he became frail and fell. After he left the hospital, he decided to go into a nursing home. We found a very good facility, one in which the residents were free to move around and have a social life. It became a real home to my father. He was quite content, he made friends, and he created a niche for himself there. That's another thing I learned. He showed me by his example that his world was inside of him. His life in the nursing home held meaning for him because of who he was inside. I learned that your self is your world; you can give up all your possessions and live in one room and still have the important things you need. It really is about your inner life, and my father's inner life was very rich. He would talk to me about his philosophy, his life, his experiences. He was very social. He loved people and could have a conversation with anyone in the nursing home. He could connect with others, and that's so important. He seemed very happy to be by himself; he liked his own company. During those last months, he shared with me his feelings about death and dying—that he wasn't afraid, that he knew he was dying. He was a very wise person.

My father died in the nursing home in my arms. He went very gently. I held him for quite a while. He was still warm, and I wanted to feel his warmth. I think because of that experience I really haven't any fear of death. And also because of that experience I am even more aware of my own mortality. Knowing that death is always there at my side doesn't take away from my life or my joy in living. I remember leaving the nursing home and thinking how thankful I was to be alive. And then I thought that I, too, could be here one day, and if I am, I will make the best of it as my father did. I will be alive, I will have myself, and my self will be enough. I now savor life much more with that awareness.

I'm sixty-eight now, the eldest in the family. Yes, I'm both older and wiser. My caregiving experiences with my mother and father have been part of my journey toward a growing self-awareness. What I've written in my book on being a caregiver for aging parents I'll say here once again: "To honor thy father and mother ultimately means that we give up impossible, self-destructive expectations. Until we learn to honor ourselves, we cannot truly honor our elderly parents."

WENDY LUSTBADER

*Wendy Lustbader is a therapist and counselor. She often
helps others deal with the stress and frustration they're
experiencing as family caregivers. Many of her clients are
members of that fast-growing population of middle-aged
children with aging parents. I asked Wendy to share some of
her thoughts and experiences in counseling family caregivers.*

A lot of people in their forties, fifties, and sixties who
haven't yet been caregivers are terrified of it. They
think, "Oh my God, what if my parents need me?
What if my older sister or brother needs me?" They think
caregiving is going to be a time of unmitigated horror and
strain. They can't see the enrichments to the self that will
accrue later. I like to tell people that there are many hidden
benefits and not to run the other way when your chance
comes. Go for it. It's being at a distance from illness, disability, or death that makes us so afraid. If you go up close to a
thing and touch it, you learn the contours of it. It's not all one

bleak world of horror. It's in service to others that we learn and grow. In the realm of the soul we are truly limitless.

One day, it was her turn to become a family caregiver. She and her husband, Barry, decided to have his very ill mother move into their home. She talked with me about some of the things she learned.

It didn't take me long before I realized that Barry and I had stopped living when my mother-in-law moved in our house. We stopped going to the movies on Saturday night. We didn't go out to dinner with each other, and our time in our own relationship had dwindled to almost nothing. I realized this wasn't going to work. So I said, "Barry, we have to go out. We have to go out on Saturday night." He said, "Oh no, we can't do that. She'll be so lonely. We just can't go out." And I said, "Barry, we can't take away her loneliness, and if we don't live while we take care of her, then we're waiting for her to die so we can live our lives again."

It's in service to others that we learn and grow. In the realm of the soul we are truly limitless.

And so, with a good deal of reluctance on my husband's part, we began making plans for Saturday nights. The first few times were very, very stressful for us. It was hard to take our lives back because it meant leaving her alone. It was painful. But after the third time we went out, she said, "Have a good time, kids," and gave us her blessing. When we'd come back from an evening out, it was good seeing her again and fun telling her what we had done and where we had gone. And there was a sense that the oxygen had come back into the house.

Near the end of her life, my mother-in-law couldn't lie down at night. The cancer in her lungs made it too hard to breathe. Three nights in a row I sat with her all night, rubbing her back. I was getting more and more exhausted. Sometimes she'd fall asleep at 4:00 or 5:00 A.M., but this one night I was at the end of my rope. I'm a very patient person, but we were like little children, both so tired and aggravated. I said, "Well, if you won't lie down, then I'm going to lie down," and I just passed out. You've got to picture this. I was sound asleep diagonally across her hospital bed. The next thing I knew, I woke up and my mother-in-law was in my arms. Certainly in our waking state we would never cuddle. But I made sure I cuddled her really well as she slept. And in all my memories of the caregiving, this was the most beautiful time. Even though she was asleep, I was very much awake, and I really got to hold her.

You learn after taking care of someone to bless literally every day that you're not homebound.

There were blessings in this experience I can hardly verbalize. I feel like I went to the edge of the wilderness and looked into it. It was a kind of wake-up call. You learn after taking care of someone to bless literally every day that you're not homebound. I feel the privilege of enjoying a beautiful day, even being able to walk up my steps. I have so many memories of helping my mother-in-law go down those very same steps, one breath at a time, one step at a time. With the cancer in her lungs, she could only take very measured steps. And in her delight in being out of the house she would see every flower, every little special garden arrangement, every pot, every little statuette. My mother-in-law taught me how to see; she conveyed delight to me. And that gift of being able to really see and slow down has stayed with me.

These observations just don't get made in the hurry of the hurly-burly life so many of us live. But the minute someone you love gets sick or suffers a devastating medical condition, you say, "Whoa, what is life about? I'm just as fragile as this person lying in the bed. What am I doing? How am I living? What is the rest of the time that I have really for?" I think in our life today we almost need illness in order to be called to life, to become fully awake.

AFTERWORD:
A CONVERSATION WITH STUDS TERKEL

*These "afterthoughts" are a bit of an author indulgence.
However, because I feel so strongly about the power of story,
I'm taking this opportunity to introduce you to Studs
Terkel, one of the great living storytellers. This ninety-year-
old Chicago-based oral historian, radio personality, writer,
and raconteur is as familiar to many of us as a favorite
piece of comfortable furniture. You may have read his books
or heard the nationally syndicated daily radio program he
broadcast for many decades, or possibly have had an
opportunity to meet him personally. Maybe you were
among the many that he has approached over the years
with a request to share your hopes, dreams, fears, and feelings. "Tell me your story," Studs has said hundreds of times
as he's turned on his tape recorder.
    I first met Studs Terkel in the late 1960s. I was just
beginning what became for me a thirty-five-year career in
educational and public radio. He was available for an
interview at the University of Minnesota where he was*

*giving a lecture. I was a fledgling reporter at the campus
radio station and was the lucky one who got the assignment.*

*Studs Terkel's writings and his conversations with me
have been, for me, the ultimate proof of the validity of the
quote by Muriel Rukeyser in the introduction to this book:
"The world isn't made of atoms, it's made of stories."
Occasionally, Studs interviews famous celebrities or well-
known personalities. He mostly collects stories of folks like
you and me. Studs calls these the stories of ordinary heroes.
Yet, there's nothing ordinary or commonplace about the
stories he collects. In the telling, these simply-told personal
tales carry deep meaning, inspiration, and hope. Others'
experiences have the power to affect us profoundly. This is
the mystical, magical power of stories: They tell us not only
about others but about ourselves. People may be of a
different race, religion, or economic status. They may be
faced with a situation that has nothing to do directly with
our lives. Yet, the feeling, determination, acceptance,
compassion, grit, and wisdom of their personal stories speak
to us. Through these stories we gain insight, courage,
comfort, and inspiration.*

*As I write these words, I've just come back from a trip
to Chicago where I visited with Studs. He invited me to
come to his home. Of course, I brought along my tape
recorder. "Can I interview the interviewer?" I asked. "Sure,
we can talk," he said. "But you know I generally don't talk
about personal things." I was aware that Ida, his wife of
sixty years, had died recently while undergoing heart
surgery. On the window ledge in the living room was an
urn holding her ashes. Next to it was a vase of yellow
daisies, her favorite flower. He repeated to me what he had
written in the introduction to his most recent book:
"Sometimes I look over at the urn and mumble, 'Whaddya
think of that, kid?'" Somewhat unwillingly, yet prodded by
his natural generosity, Studs began to talk about Ida.*

She was eighty-seven when she died. We were married sixty years. For me Ida wasn't an old woman. She was that girl, that social worker in a maroon smock, that I first saw all those years ago when I was doing some work for the WPA during the Great Depression. She would listen to clients tell their troubles. Ida was so open that people were just drawn to her. I learned that from her—a certain kind of awareness of others, a recognition of their feelings. She was like a dancer—light and delicate, yet strong. I remember what the poet Gwendolyn Brooks, who knew her well, said of Ida: "She could dance on a moonbeam." There was a wonderful grace about her. When she fell down, she'd say, "I fall gracefully." She bore pain gracefully. Even after her sense of taste was completely gone, we'd be at a dinner party and there would be an easiness about her. Like I say, there was a grace about her.

This is the mystical, magical power of stories:
They tell us not only about others but about ourselves.

Ida had a heart valve operation and a bovine valve replacement many years ago. After fifteen years it just wore out and there was a leakage. The doctors wanted to have surgery quickly. I think back, and I believe I talked her into the surgery. I remember the night before the operation she said, "I want to go home." She was really against having the surgery. I guess this is my confession that I should have listened to Ida and heard what she was saying. She was ready to go, yet she never, never complained. She knew she was dying. She wanted to go home. I don't think I'll say much more about Ida. I don't talk much about personal things.

Studs looked pensively at the urn on the window ledge. I recall there was a brief silence. We continued our conversation on another subject.

My last book, *Will the Circle Be Unbroken*, is about death, but it's really about life. A guy called me from Kansas City. He had read my book and was affected by one particular story about the illness and death of a loved one. He had lost his companion, and he told me that reading stories about other people dealing with sickness, suffering, and loss was a healing experience for him. Now he may go out and tell others his story and have an effect on someone else. People get insights this way.

I remember a story I included in an early book I did called *Working*. I had talked with this wonderful waitress, and she told me about her day working at this steak house— the varicose veins, the headaches, and the exhaustion at the end of the day. Why was a middle-aged woman a waitress? She needed the cash, her daughter was in trouble, her son was on drugs, her husband had left her. One day, a man stopped me on the street. He said, "I read your book and I want to tell you how I feel about that story of the waitress. I'm never going to speak to a waitress like I've done before." He had never seen life from her point of view. I had touched him, and his behavior.

Reading stories about other people dealing with sickness, suffering, and loss was a healing experience.

Here's something I learned from Ida. It's about truth. When you do a book, you choose people who have a certain insight, a kind of way of saying things that other people feel but can't say. They tell the truth of their experiences and feelings. How do I find them? Sometimes it's accidental, sometimes people tell me about someone they know, and sometimes it's someone I know.

One time after I had done a radio broadcast about race relations, a woman called me. She was furious. In a very upset tone she told me, "You're so smug, so righteous about your liberal attitudes. You remind me of my mother." Now that interested me so I asked for her mother's phone number. The conversation I ended up having with her mother turned out to be an excellent interview that I included in one of my books. She was wonderful. Then one time I got into a taxi, and the driver asked me if I had seen the movie *Lord Jim*. He was talking about the film based on Joseph Conrad's novel. And he said, "Well, that movie is about me. It's about a guy who was a coward all his life and suddenly found his courage. That's me." I sensed it was a story too good to miss. I turned on my tape recorder. So there you are. You never know.

What we do here on this earth, what we say here—our stories— stay here when we're gone.

Like I told you earlier, the book that just came out is about death, but it's really about life. James Joyce wrote in *Finnegan's Wake*, "You really accept death when you recognize the permanence of life." What people do and say can have permanence. Maybe the stories of others I tell will have a continuing life. One guy who read my book called me up and talked about how deeply he had been affected by the story I told. Now he may have an effect on someone else. What we do here on this earth, what we say here—our stories—stay here when we're gone.

Sometimes the answers we seek come from unexpected places. This very morning I was going through a collection of notes and clippings that I planned to file weeks ago but never got around to. As I was sorting, I wasn't totally concentrating on what I was doing. My thoughts were on writing the conclusion to this afterword. I wanted to leave you, the reader, with a few words of inspiration, encouragement, and insight. Quite unexpectedly, I found the very words I needed scribbled on one of the papers I was sorting.

About five years ago, I had read a book by Jean Shinoda Bolen entitled Close to the Bone. *She had written extensively and eloquently about life-threatening illness and the search for meaning. The book was impressive, and I had taken many notes. Now, here on the back of an envelope, I found one of them. Bolen had quoted from a children's book by Barry Lopez called* Crow and Weasel *the following words. I leave you with Lopez's wisdom and insight.*

"If stories come to you, care for them. And learn to give them away where they are needed. Sometimes a person needs a story more than food to stay alive."